BENJAMIN ELLIOTT JONES–A KENTUCKY MILITIAMAN IN THE SECOND WAR OF AMERICA'S INDEPENDENCE 1812-1815

Also By Gary C. Cole

Across the Frontier
12 APRIL
Three Hundred and Sixty-six Days at Fort Delaware
Riding With The 19th Texas Cavalry In The War West
Of The Mississippi 1862-1865

BENJAMIN ELLIOTT JONES–A KENTUCKY MILITIAMAN IN THE SECOND WAR OF AMERICA'S INDEPENDENCE 1812-1815

Gary C. Cole

To my wife Jestine
and
my great-great-great grandfather Benjamin Elliott Jones
who honorably served in Micah Taul's Company of Infantry,
Seventh Regiment, Kentucky Militia in The Second War
of America's Independence

1812 U.S. Flag

Contents

Illustrations

Acknowledgements

Any historical work such as this is indebted to those who have gone before and produced the historical record on which it is based. Without them, this story about Benjamin Elliott Jones–a militiaman in the Second War of America's Independence–could not have been told. To them, I am extremely grateful.

Rodes Garth–a Private in Micah Taul's Company of Infantry, Seventh Regiment, Kentucky Militia–kept a journal of daily events during most of his six-month term of service with Taul's Company and preserved much of the historical record about the role of Taul's Company during the War of 1812. His journal is extensively referenced in this book.

Micah Taul–Captain of Micah Taul's Company of Infantry, Seventh Regiment, Kentucky Militia–wrote his Memoirs after the war which were published posthumously by the Kentucky State Historical Society in 1939 and add to the historical record about the role of Taul's Company in the War of 1812.

Deana Woolfolk–a genealogist and wife of David Costner, a distant cousin of mine in Orlando, Florida–discovered and recorded much of what we know about Rev. Elliott Jones, Benjamin Elliott Jones, and related families. Her records were invaluable in telling this story about Benjamin Elliott Jones.

Nancy Cole Douglas–a genealogist and my cousin in Azle, Texas–assisted with the discovery and evaluation of information about Rev. Elliott Jones, Benjamin Elliott Jones, and related families referenced in this book.

Jestine Cole–my wife–encouraged me to finish this book and assisted with illustrations and final proof reading.

Foreword

"Those who have gone before cry out for us to tell their story."

Some twenty-nine years after Great Britain recognized the independence of its former colonies, the United States declared war on Great Britain on 18 June 1812. More than 458,400 militiamen would ultimately serve in the U.S. forces during that war which would be fought on the high seas, the Atlantic seaboard, the Great Lakes, Chesapeake Bay, the Canadian border, throughout the U.S. Northwest Territory, and in the Southern Frontier of the Gulf South. At the war's beginning, the United States planned to quickly invade Canada, seize Canadian territory, and force Great Britain to negotiate a peace favorable to the U.S., but it didn't work out that way. Brigadier General William Hull invaded Upper Canada soon after the war began, but was forced to surrender Fort Detroit, the surrounding village of some 700 settlers, and the entire Army of the Northwest on 16 August 1812. The Michigan Territory was then declared to be part of Great Britain and Shawnee Indian Chief Tecumseh increased his attacks against American settlers in the territory.

Eight days after the fall of Fort Detroit, a militia company was formed in Wayne County, Kentucky to fight the British and their Indian allies in the Indiana territory. At the call for volunteers, Benjamin Elliott Jones volunteered to serve six months as a Private in Captain Micah Taul's Company, Seventh Regiment, Kentucky Militia and was eager to fight the British and their Indian allies in what many considered to be the Second War of America's Independence.

Taul's Company left Monticello, Kentucky on 24 August 1812 and marched to the Cumberland River where it encamped for the night unaware that Fort Detroit had been captured by the British.

Two days later, the Company learned that Fort Detroit had fallen to the British and the Company's route of march was changed to the Northwest.

The story of Benjamin Elliott Jones' military service with Micah Taul's Militia Company is a story of seemingly endless marching and searching for an opportunity to engage the British and their Indian allies in battle–an opportunity that never came.

When the term of service for the militiamen of Taul's Company was about to end on 22 March 1813, the Company was marched from St. Marys to Cincinnati, paid, and discharged. The Company arrived home on 21 March and the militiamen were treated as heroes even though they never met the British and their Indian allies in battle. Benjamin would spend the rest of the war in Monticello struggling to follow the war's progress. He eagerly sought news about the battles fought and celebrated the victories won and agonized over the defeats suffered.

Benjamin celebrated the end of the war in February 1815 and remembered with pride his role in that war–how he fought with Revolutionary War Veterans and the sons of such Veterans in the Second War of America's Independence–and regretted that he never had an opportunity to fight the British and their Indian allies.

Some three years after the war ended, Benjamin left Wayne County, Kentucky and migrated some 300 miles south and settled in Lawrence County, Alabama. He later moved to Fayette County, Alabama and lived there for the rest of his life. He was living in Fayette County when Alabama seceded from the Union on 11 January 1861; he was living there when the Confederacy was formed at Montgomery, Alabama in February; he was living there when the great War for Southern Independence began on 12 April 1861; and he saw his family experience the hardships and horrors of a nation at war with itself.

Benjamin struggled with his family's allegiance to both sides during the war and sought news about the war's progress just as he had followed the progress of America's Second War of Independence, but he did not live to see the end of the great war because he died on 19 January 1863 some 27 months before General Robert E. Lee formally surrendered his Army of Northern Virginia on 12 April 1865 at the village of Appomattox Courthouse in Virginia.

Jones Gravestone

1

WAR

At the dawn of the 19th Century, Great Britain and France were engulfed by their war in Europe which began when France declared war on Great Britain on 1 February 1793. As the war progressed, each country increasingly sought to restrict the international trade of the other. The British Parliament passed a series of Orders-in-Council which forbid trade with France and any ship bound for a French port was subject to search and seizure. [1] The British placed a blockade on the French islands in the Caribbean and on some 800 miles of the coast of Europe from Brest, Germany to Elbe, France. [2] Napoleon responded with his Berlin Degree on 21 November 1806. The Degree enacted a blockade of the British Isles and forbid all trade with Great Britain. Any ship sailing from a British port was seized; its cargo was confiscated; and its sailors became prisoners of war.[3] The United States had the largest neutral merchant marine fleet in the world, traded extensively with Europe, and got caught up in the conflict between Great Britain and France. Great Britain seized 528 U.S. flag ships between 1803 and 1807 and 206 U.S. flag ships were seized by the French.[4]

Great Britain ignored its former colonies' claims of neutrality, effectively dismissed their status as an independent sovereign nation, and impressed American sailors. [5] The British did not recognize the right of an individual to relinquish his British citizenship and become a citizen of another country. The British Navy considered an American sailor subject to impressment if he was born British. As its war with France progressed, Great Britain faced a shortage of skilled sailors and stopped and searched American ships anywhere in the world. British ships were often stationed just outside U.S. harbors, stopped and searched ships entering and leaving the harbors, and U.S. sailors were forcibly recruited into the British Navy. [6]

British soldiers occupied several forts in the Northwest Territory in violation of the Treaty of Paris [7] and supplied arms to Native American tribes who raided settlers throughout the territory. Years of increasingly angry diplomacy failed and the United States declared war on Great Britain on 18 June 1812. On 9 January of the following year, Great Britain declared war on the United States. The war would last two years and eight months and would be fought on the high seas, the Atlantic Seaboard, the Great Lakes, the Chesapeake Bay, along the Canadian border, in the U.S. Northwest Territory, and in the U.S. territories in the Gulf South.[8]

Neither side was prepared to fight the war when it began. Most of Great Britain's 240,000-man army was heavily engaged in its war with France in Europe. Britain only had 5,200 regular troops in Canada supported by some 4,000 Canadian militiamen and Britain's Indian allies which would ultimately number 10,000-15,000 warriors. By war's end, Britain's regular troops in North America would number more than 48,100 soldiers. When the war began, the United States Army with 7,000 soldiers was larger than the British army in North America. By war's end, the U.S. Army would number some 35,800 troops and an unbelievable 458,463 militiamen would have participated in the war.[9]

The United States Navy had 7,250 sailors and marines with 22 commissioned vessels when the war began. [10] Great Britain's Royal Navy was the largest, most powerful navy in the world. It had 85 ships in American waters at the beginning of the war and those ships were destined to play a major role in the conflict. The U. S. Navy's principal fighting force was a squadron of three frigates and two sloops of war and was incapable of engaging the British fleet in battle on the open seas, but the Americans would successfully engage the British in one-on-one ship combat. [11]

Not all Americans supported the war. The Northeastern States opposed it and refused to provide financial support and militia for the war. Delegates from Connecticut, Massachusetts, New Hampshire, Rhode Island, and Vermont would meet at the Hartford Convention 15 December 1814 – 5 January 1815 to discuss their dissatisfaction with the war's progress. Some delegates even suggested that the Northeastern States exercise their Constitutional right to secede from the Union and enter into a separate peace and trade alliance with Great Britain.[12]

Although the U.S. was ill-prepared to fight the war it started, some preparations actually began in February 1812 when President James Madison named Michigan Territory Governor William Hull Brigadier General and appointed him commander of the yet-to-be raised Army of the Northwest.

William Hull had been appointed Governor and Indian Agent of the Michigan Territory on 22 March 1805 which was then occupied by native American Indians, except for two small settlements at Fort Detroit and Fort Michilimackinac. In 1807 Hull successfully negotiated the Treaty of Detroit with four Indian tribes which ceded to the United States most of the territory of southeast Michigan and northwestern Ohio to the mouth of Ohio's Maumee River, but Indian depredations continued. [13]

President Madison ordered General Hull to raise an Army of the Northwest and go to Fort Detroit with its frontier settlement of some 700 settlers and protect it from the British and their Indian allies.[14] Fort Detroit had been established by the French in 1701 on the west bank of the Detroit River to control the fur trade in the central part of North America and prevent British colonists from moving west into the territory. The Fort was ceded to the British in 1760 during the French and Indian War and the British surrendered the Fort to the United States on 11 July 1796 under terms of the Jay Treaty which resolved issues remaining after the Treaty of Paris ended the Revolutionary War. A fire destroyed most of Fort Detroit in 1805 and Fort Lernoult was built a few hundred yards north of the burned fort and renamed 'Fort Detroit.' [15]

General Hull left Washington, D.C. and traveled to Ohio whose governor was raising a 1,200-man militia and arrived in Cincinnati on 10 May 1812. Fifteen days later, he took command of the three-regiment militia at Dayton and marched the regiments to Urbana, Ohio where the militia was joined by a fourth regiment of some 300 soldiers–the 4th Regiment of Vincennes, Indiana Territory. Hull left Urbana and marched his Army of the Northwest overland through the Ohio wilderness towards Fort Detroit where he planned to begin his invasion of Upper Canada. [16]

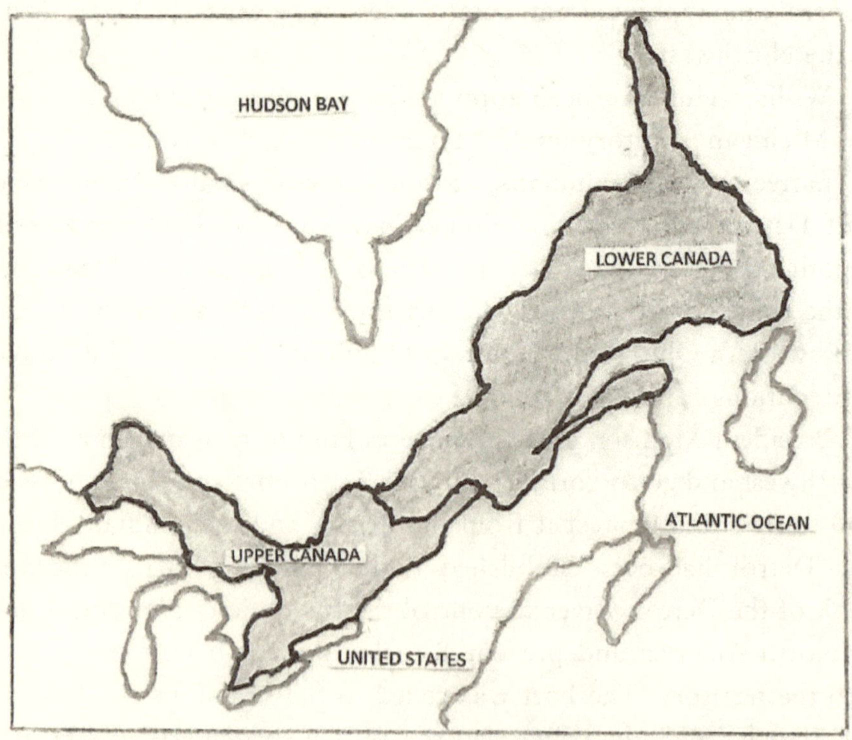

Upper & Lower Canada in 1791

2

INVASION OF UPPER CANADA

By the end of June, General Hull's command reached the rapids of the Maumee River and Hull made the first of several critical mistakes he would make during his invasion of Canada. Hull was unaware that the United States had declared war on Great Britain and chartered the schooner *Cuyahoga Packet* to sail ahead of his army to Fort Detroit with his personal baggage and papers. The schooner had to sail on the British-controlled Detroit River and pass the British Fort Amherstburg whose commander was aware that Great Britain was at war with the United States. When the *Cuyahoga Packet* passed the fort, it was captured by the British and Hull's personal papers mentioning his fear of Indians and outlining his plans to invade Canada and capture Fort Amherstburg were found. While Hull's army of some 2,000 soldiers was struggling to cut a road through the Ohio wilderness, Fort Amherstburg was being strengthened in anticipation of Hull's attack. [17]

General Hull arrived at Fort Detroit on 5 July and a week later began his invasion of Upper Canada without some two hundred Ohio militiamen who refused to leave American territory. [18] The rest of Hull's army crossed the Detroit River on 12 July 1812, captured the village of Sandwich without opposition, and the village became his base of operations for his invasion of Canada. Hull issued a proclamation to the Canadian citizens that he had invaded Canada to offer them peace, liberty, and security, but the Canadians did not respond well to his proclamation and it increased their resistance to Hull and his invasion.[19]

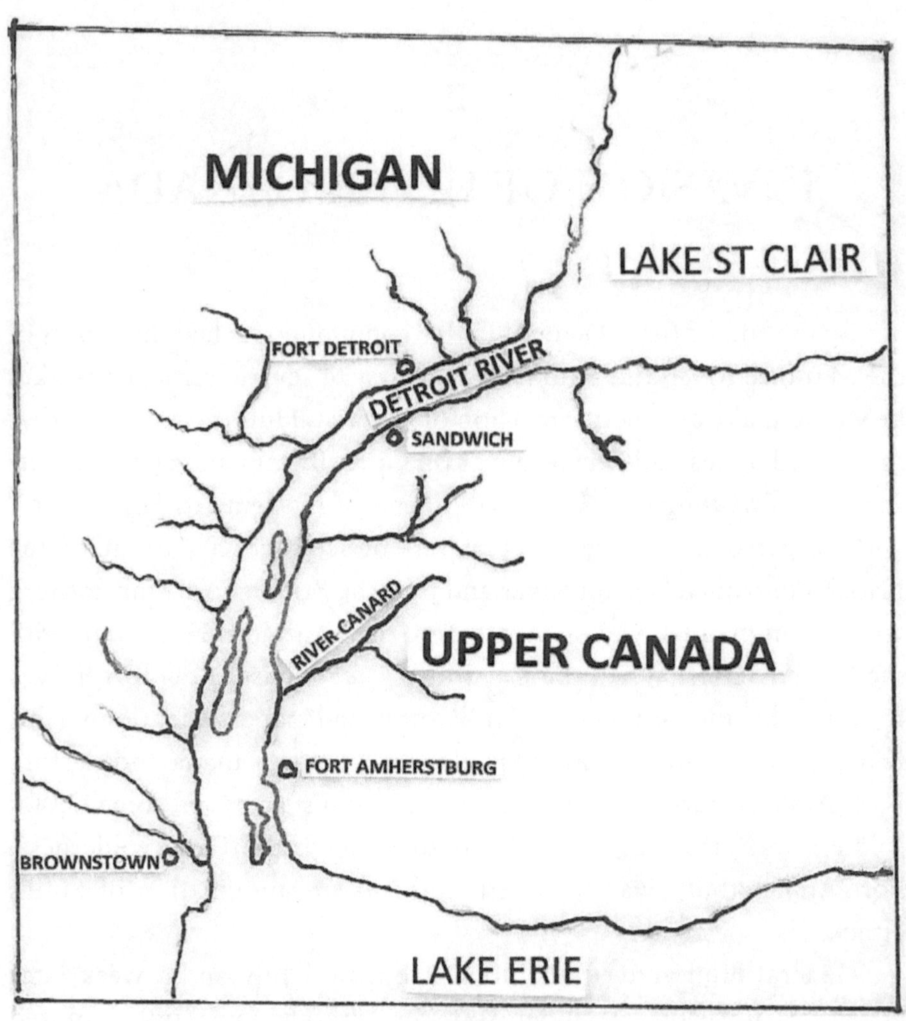

Detroit River

Hull marched his army south along the Detroit River towards Fort Amherstburg which had been built in 1796 by the British on the east side of the Detroit River near where it empties into Lake Erie to replace Fort Detroit which had been ceded to the United States under the terms of the Jay Treaty. Fort Amherstburg was the only British garrison along the Detroit River and was headquarters of the British Indian Department which secured the allegiance of the Indian tribes in the Northwest Territory by giving them weapons, ammunition, food, cloth, tools, and other supplies. With few roads in the region, the Fort provided the only reliable line of communication for commerce and the military. [20]

Hull never reached Fort Amherstburg. On 16 July, he was attacked by a small British patrol from the Fort at the Canard River. Hull thought that the British force was much larger than it was and abandoned his plans to capture the Fort and retreated to his base of operations at the village of Sandwich. [21]

When General Hull learned that Fort Michilimackinac on the Straits of Mackinac between Lake Michigan and Lake Huron had been captured by a force of some 600 British regulars, fur traders, and Indians on 17 July without a shot being fired, [22] he ordered Fort Dearborn to be evacuated and it would be on 15 August. The small garrison with women and children left the Fort early that morning and were attacked soon after they left the protection of the Fort by 500 Pottawattomie Indians. Half of the Americans were killed and the other half were captured. [23]

The fall of Fort Michilimackinac and the decision by some of the Indians who helped capture the Fort to head south to join Shawnee Chief Tecumseh at Fort Amherstburg struck fear in Hull's heart. He knew that the fall of the Fort would embolden the Indians and feared that it would unleash a horde of Indians from the north. [24]

Hull sent Major Thomas Van Horn with 200 soldiers to Brownstown Creek south of Detroit on 5 August to pick up cattle and supplies and escort them back to Fort Detroit. When Hull learned that Tecumseh had ambushed and massacred half of Van Horn's force, Hull feared that his army then at the village of Sandwich would be attacked by the Indians. He decided to abandon his invasion of Canada and retreat to the safety of Fort Detroit. Hull crossed to the American side of the Detroit River and arrived at the Fort on 8 August 1812, but it would not be as safe as he envisioned.[25]

3

FALL OF FORT DETROIT

British Major General Sir Isaac Brock was transferred to Canada in 1802 from a distinguished military career fighting Napoleon in Europe and began improving Canada's defenses. Eight years later in 1810, he became commander of all British forces in Upper Canada. [26] When U.S. Brigadier General William Hull invaded Upper Canada in July 1812, Brock decided he needed to reassure Canadian settlers and Britain's Indian allies that Great Britain was strong enough to thwart Hull's advance into Canada.[27] Brock ordered the successful British attack on Fort Michilimackinc on 17 July 1812 and decided to go on the offensive against Hull and his invasion force. Brock arrived at Fort Amherstburg on 13 August and became its commander with some 300 regular British soldiers, 400 Canadian militiamen, and 600 Indian warriors led by Chief Tecumseh.[28] Brock and Tecumseh formed an alliance and planned to seize Fort Detroit and they did.

Three days after his arrival at Fort Amherstburg, Brock crossed to the American side of the Detroit River and advanced towards Fort Detroit while it was being bombarded by two British gunboats on the Detroit River and the artillery battery he had placed along the shore of the river at the village of Sandwich.[29] Brock sent a message to General Hull stating that a large Indian force was approaching the Fort and he would be unable to control the savage warriors once the fighting began. Brock demanded that Hull surrender the Fort, but Hull refused.[30]

When Hull saw the large British and Indian force gathering around Fort Detroit early the next morning on 16 August, he panicked and lost all hope of defending the Fort and settlement.[31] He surrendered Fort Detroit, the surrounding village of 700 settlers, and the 2,500 soldiers in the Army of the Northwest to 1,330 British regulars and 600 Indian warriors.[32] Hull later said that he lacked enough gunpowder and other supplies to withstand a siege of the fort, but the British reported that they captured sixty barrels of gunpowder and enough other materiel to withstand a lengthy siege [33]

General Hull would be court marshaled in 1814 for cowardice and neglect of duty in surrendering Fort Detroit and was sentenced to die by a firing squad, but President Madison commuted Hull's sentence because of his meritorious service during the Revolutionary War. He had joined a local militia company at the outbreak of fighting in that war and was promoted to captain then rose through the ranks of the Continental Army to Lieutenant Colonel. He had fought with distinction in eight major battles of the war and was recognized by Commanding General George Washington and the Second Continental Congress for his service during the war.[34]

The fall of Fort Detroit was a stunning victory for the British and a humiliating defeat for the United States. The Michigan Territory was declared to be part of Great Britain and Tecumseh increased his attacks against American settlers in the territory.[35]

4

SETTLEMENT OF KENTUCKY

The threat of Indian attacks against settlers on America's frontier was nothing new to Americans. Some of the most hazardous and bloody events in America's history occurred during the settlement of Kentucky from the mid-18th century to the early part of the 19th century. Thousands of settlers were killed in skirmishes with the Indians who were determined to protect their hunting grounds against the encroachment of the white man, but the white man kept coming.[36] Settlements west of the Appalachian Mountains grew rapidly after 1775 with settlers migrating from Virginia, North Carolina, and Pennsylvania to Kentucky via the Ohio River, the Cumberland Gap, the Wilderness Road, and Boone's Trace despite threats of Indian attacks.[37] Among the early settlers migrating from Virginia were Dawson Wade, Sr., Robert Wallace, and Reverend Elliott Jones. The men became close friends and their families intermarried.

The area that became Kentucky was part of Augusta County, Virginia which was formed 1738-1745 and designated as Kentucky County, Virginia in December 1776. The county was divided into three counties in 1780–Fayette, Jefferson, and Lincoln–and those three counties were divided into nine counties in 1790 and those nine counties were further divided thereafter.[38]

As the settlements in Kentucky grew, the settlers became dissatisfied with Virginia and efforts began to separate Kentucky from Virginia. The threat of Indian attacks was a daily reality for the Kentucky settlers and local militia could not be used to defend the settlers against the Indians without authorization by the Virginia Governor and that authorization was difficult to obtain on a timely basis. Traveling to the Virginia Capitol was a long and dangerous journey and legal matters were difficult to handle. Trade along the Mississippi River was vital to Kentucky's economy, but trade with the Spanish colony of New Orleans was forbidden by Virginia's government. These and other problems fueled dissatisfaction with Virginia and a series of constitutional conventions were held in Kentucky beginning in 1784 to explore separation from Virginia. A proposal for Kentucky to secede from both Virginia and the United States failed, but efforts to separate Kentucky from Virginia continued. In 1788, Virginia finally consented to Kentucky's separation and it became the 15th State of the Union on 1 June 1792.[39]

Dawson Wade, Sr. had explored Kentucky with Daniel Boone [40] in 1767–nine years before the Revolutionary War.[41] Wade was a soldier in that war between 1775 and 1778 and left Virginia in 1784 with his wife Rachael Burnside and their children and migrated to Kentucky. They travelled along the Wilderness Road and settled at McGee's Station in what would become Clark County in 1792 and Montgomery County in 1796. He had served in Captain Looney's Militia Company in Botetourt County, Virginia from 1770-1783 to protect settlers from Indian attacks on the Virginia frontier and became Captain of the 34th Militia Regiment in Montgomery County, Kentucky on 8 May 1802 to help protect Kentucky settlers from hostile Indians.[42]

Robert Wallace had also served in the militia in Virginia–John Murray's Company of Volunteers in Botetourt County–to help protect settlers in the Virginia wilderness from Indian attacks and was also a soldier in the Revolutionary War. He moved to Kentucky with his wife Jane McHenry and their children around 1785 and received a 1,000-acre Land Grant surveyed on 11 March 1786. He joined the militia–Adair's Militia Regiment in 1793 and Russell's Battalion

Mounted Volunteers in 1794–to help protect Kentucky settlers from Indian attacks. He moved to Wayne County, Kentucky shortly before it was formed in 1800 from Pulaski and Cumberland counties and the 1810 Census for the county reflected that he owned two slaves. In 1811, he acquired 133 acres between Beaver Creek and Otter Creek in Wayne County.[43]

Reverend Elliott Jones left Virginia sometime prior to 1787 and settled in Fayette County, Kentucky where he married Elizabeth Wade–the daughter of Dawson Wade, Sr. and Rachel Burnside on 25 May 1788.[44] He moved to Wayne County, Kentucky prior to 27 May 1801–the date he performed the first recorded marriage in the county. He would perform all but two of the marriages in the county during the next ten years. [45] Elliott's son Benjamin Elliott Jones married Robert Wallace's daughter Viney on 3 November 1811. He became a militiaman like his grandfather Dawson Wade Sr. and his father-in-law Robert Wallace and would leave Wayne County the following August to fight the British and their Indian allies in the Second War of America's Independence–the War of 1812. [46]

Marriage Consent

5

WAYNE COUNTY MILITIA

Eight days after the fall of Fort Detroit on 16 August 1812, a Kentucky militia company was raised by Captain Micah Taul in Wayne County, Kentucky to fight the British and their Indian allies in the Indiana Territory. At the call for volunteers on 23 August 1812, Benjamin Elliott Jones volunteered to serve for six months as a Private in Captain Micah Taul's Company of Infantry, Seventh Regiment, Kentucky Militia–Colonel Joshua Barbee's Regiment.[47] At the time of his enlistment, Benjamin was described as 5'-6" tall with dark hair, blue eyes, and tolerably fair complexion."[48] Most of the volunteers in Taul's Company were Revolutionary War Veterans or sons of such Veterans.[49] Benjamin Jones was neither.

Benjamin was born on 26 March 1790 after the Revolutionary War in what would become Wayne County, Kentucky ten years later when the county was formed out of Pulaski and Cumberland Counties and named for Revolutionary War Hero General "Mad" Anthony Wayne. Benjamin's father Reverend Elliott Jones–born in 1764 in the Virginia Colony, British America–was twelve years old when the colonies signed their Declaration of Independence and was seventeen years old when the last major battle of the war was fought at Yorktown. However, Benjamin's grandfather Dawson Wade, Sr.–born 1732 in the Virginia Colony of British America–was a Revolutionary War soldier between 1775 and 1778 and Benjamin must have grown up hearing his stories about the war and America's fight for its independence. He would have been honored to serve with the war's veterans and their sons who were eager to fight the British in what many considered to be the Second War of America's Independence.

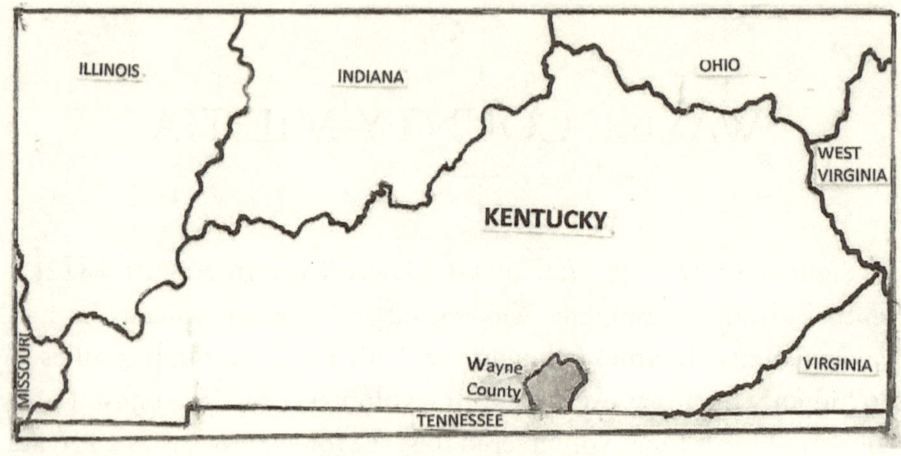

Wayne County, Kentucky

Captain Taul's Company left Monticello, Kentucky on 24 August 1812 and marched to the Cumberland River where it encamped for the night, unaware that Fort Detroit had been captured by the British on 16 August 1812. The Company continued its march on the 25th and encamped at Maple Swamp. [50] That same day, William Henry Harrison, who would become the 9th President of the United States in 1841, was elected Major General of the Kentucky militia [51] and the militiamen in Taul's Company must have been excited to serve under him.

Harrison had become extremely popular with Kentuckians after he defeated the Shawnee Indians at the Tippecanoe River on 7 November 1811. He had assembled an army of 950 territorial militia and regular army infantry during the summer of 1811 and marched up the Wabash River from Vincennes to the Indian village of Prophetstown near the Tippecanoe River. He arrived at the village on 6 November and met with the Indians in a peaceful meeting, but the warriors launched a surprise attack on Harrison's army at 4:00 a.m. the next morning. Harrison had anticipated the possibility of such an attack and was well prepared. His men went to bed fully armed and ready for combat. Harrison's army defeated the Indians in vicious hand-to-hand combat that lasted more than two hours in the dark. The Indians were scattered across the border into Canada and their village and crops were burned. The battle significantly weakened the intertribal alliance promoted by Chief Tecumseh and his brother Tenskwatawa against the settlers in the Great Lakes region of the United States and Harrison became a folk hero in Kentucky and the rest of the nation. [52]

Taul's Company marched through Stanford on 26 August, arrived at Danville that evening, and met Captain James Barbee's Company—one of the additional six companies in Colonel Joshua Barbee's Regiment. The two companies marched five miles beyond Danville and camped before returning through Danville the next day and encamping at Fisher's Pond on the road to Newport. [53] While there, they received news that General Hull had surrendered Fort Detroit to the British on 16 August. It had been a terrible defeat for the Americans. Hull had surrendered the fort, the surrounding village of some 700 settlers, and the entire Army of the Northwest and without firing a shot. The Michigan Territory came under British control and the Indians were emboldened to increase their raids against settlers throughout the territory.

Taul's Company continued its march the next day–28 August 1812–and camped with Captain James Barbee's Company near Nicholasville in Jessamine County. The two companies continued their march on the 29th and camped that evening on the road to Frankfort. The next day, the companies received orders to change their route of march from the Indiana Territory to the Northwest due to the surrender of Fort Detroit and camped on the road to Georgetown. They arrived at Georgetown the next evening and left there 1 September and camped at Little Eagle, Dry Ridge, and

Brumbacks before camping on Banklick Creek at the foot of the forty-mile-long Dry Ridge on 4 September.[54]

The companies continued their march on 5 September and saw groups of settlers leaving the Ohio frontier for the safety of Kentucky or Virginia. Taul's militiamen considered the men leaving the frontier with their families to be cowards who should have remained and protected their homes against the British and their Indian allies. [55] The fleeing of the settlers from their homes must have strengthened the resolve of Benjamin Jones and the rest of the Kentucky militiamen to drive the Indians from the frontier and engage their British allies in combat.

The two companies arrived at Newport opposite Cincinnati on 5 September and camped along the bank of the Ohio River. The other five companies in Colonel Joshua Barbee's Regiment arrived at Newport on 6 September and the regiment drilled daily at Newport until 13 September when the regiment crossed the Ohio River, marched through Cincinnati, and travelled ten miles on the road to Dayton and camped for the night.[56]

While encamped on the road to Dayton, Barbee's Regiment received news from Boston, Massachusetts that Captain Isaac Hull, commander of the *USS Constitution*, arrived in port on 29 August with some 200 prisoners of war and reported that the frigate *USS Constitution* had defeated the British frigate *HMS Guerriere* in a single-ship encounter and sunk it some four hundred miles southeast of Halifax, Nova Scotia on 19 August 1812.[57]

The *USS Constitution* had been at Annapolis on Chesapeake Bay when the war with Great Britain began and was ordered by U. S. Secretary of the Navy Paul Hamilton to cruise off New York and protect American merchant ships against the British fleet. Some three weeks later, the *Constitution* put out to sea, headed to New York, and sighted the *HMS Guerriere*. The British ship was part of a five-ship squadron pursuing the *Constitution* which pumped most of its drinking water overboard to lighten he ship and help it pull away from the British ships. With a lightened ship and favorable winds, the *Constitution* eluded the British squadron and sailed for Boston. Two days later on 19 August 1812, the *Constitution* left Boston with a replenished water supply and sailed for Bermuda where it was again sighted by the *Guerierre*. The British ship gave chase and both ships prepared for battle.[58]

The two ships closed to within a few hundred yards of each other; moved most of their guns to one side of the ships and exchanged broadsides. The *Guerriere's* foremast and main mast were broken off at the deck in the attack, rendering the ship helpless and rolling heavily in the rough sea. The *Guerriere* surrendered and Hull planned to tow the captured ship to Boston as a war prize, but the next morning, it was determined that the ship could not be salvaged. The British crew of some 200 sailors was taken off the ship and it was set on fire and exploded. [59]

Captain Hull wanted the American public to know about his impressive victory and returned to Boston on 29 August with the captured British sailors to share the news. The American land campaign against Canada had not gone well in 1812 and the news about the *USS Constitution's* victory over the *HMS Guerriere*–one of the most active British ships stopping and searching American ships– boosted American morale and a renewed sense of patriotism spread across the Nation. [60] The Kentucky militiamen shared the enthusiasm about the *Constitution's* capture of one of the best ships in the British Navy and were proud to be Americans.

Benjamin Jones and the rest of Colonel Barbee's Regiment continued their march towards Fort Piqua on 14-15 September, passed through the small town of Lebanon, and arrived at another small town–Dayton–some fifty-seven miles north of Cincinnati on 16 September. [61] Taul's Company encountered an elderly lady a few miles from Lebanon who gave them a pail of buttermilk and asked if they were from Kentucky. Taul said they were and she replied: "May God bless ye & prosper ye, & give ye health and strength to defend the Country. Brave Kentuckians, we know you are real men of stout hearts, who will not run & leave the frontier unprotected, like our own cowardly men have done." [62]

The elderly lady was not alone in her high regard for the militiamen from Kentucky. The extraordinary fighting ability and distinguished bravery of Kentucky militiamen had long been well-recognized. At the beginning of the war, many believed that the successful invasion of Canada would be a relatively easy process. Speaker of the House Henry Clay, one of the most prominent war hawks in the U.S. Congress, declared that the "militiamen of Kentucky were capable of capturing Upper Canada and Montreal without any assistance." [63] Benjamin Jones had joined a well-respected company of militiamen whose fighting ability was unquestioned and he was now on his way to the Northwest to fight the British and their Indian allies.

Barbee's Regiment left Dayton on 17 September and headed to Fort Piqua on the Miami River. The Fort–a small stockade supply post with a single blockhouse in the center of the stockade–had been built by General "Mad" Anthony Wayne in 1794. [64]

General Harrison was appointed Major General and named the commander of the second Army of the Northwest on 17 September and was ordered to retake Fort Detroit and end the Indian menace in the Michigan Territory. The second Army of the Northwest would be a sizeable army expected to number some 10,000 soldiers and would include the Kentucky, Indiana, and Ohio militias, regular army soldiers, rangers, and volunteers, and troops from Pennsylvania and Virginia. [65]

General Harrison planned to conduct a fall campaign to retake Fort Detroit, but soon learned that the heavy autumn rains would saturate the ground to the point that it would be impossible to move a large army overland with its heavy guns, supplies, and rations. The effort to retake the Fort would have to wait until winter when the rivers and lake shores would freeze and support the movement of his army. [66]

Colonel Barbee's Regiment passed through Staunton on the 18th on its way to Fort Piqua, crossed the Miami River, and camped at Troy near the banks of the river. The Regiment arrived at Fort Piqua on the 19th and two days later, Taul's Company received orders to leave the Fort the next morning to escort some 200 head of cattle some 30 miles through the wilderness to St. Marys. [67] Taul would later describe the duty of escorting convoys as a "hard and disagreeable duty."

On the way to St. Marys, Taul's Company met a large number of Ohio and Kentucky troops returning from Fort Wayne with news about the siege of the Fort. The Indians had grown increasingly bitter about the presence of settlers in the Territory after their defeat at the Battle of Tippecanoe and began launching attacks against smaller U.S. forts in the territory. Fort Wayne was one of those forts. It had fallen into disrepair [68] during the decade and a half since General "Mad" Anthony Wayne built the fort after the final battle of the Northwestern Indian War–the Battle of Fallen Timbers–on 20 August 1794 which ended major hostilities in the territory until the War of 1812. [69]

The troops returning from Fort Wayne reported that warriors from the Potawatomi and Miami tribes began to gather around Fort Wayne in the early part of September and attacked the Fort on 5 September. The warriors burned settler's homes surrounding the Fort and began a siege of the Fort until 11 September when Chief Winamac's warriors attempted another attack on the Fort and suffered high casualties. The Indians broke off their attack on the 12th, crossed the Maumee River, and retreated into Ohio and the Michigan Territory.[70] Benjamin must have wished that he had been at Fort Wayne to fight the British and their Indian allies and looked forward to the day he would meet them in battle.

Taul's Company continued its march towards St. Marys on Tuesday 22 September and camped that evening at Fort Loramie on the Loramie River.[71] Fort Loramie had been built in 1795 by General "Mad" Anthony Wayne as a blockhouse with storage buildings to supply northern Ohio forts including Fort Adams, Fort Defiance, and Fort Wayne to protect the settlers against a confederation of hostile Indian tribes active in the area. The Indians and their British allies were still active in the area during the War of 1812 and the fort still served as a supply depot. [72]

Taul's Company left Fort Loramie on 23 September, delivered the cattle to St. Marys later that day, and camped that night at the site of old Fort St. Marys on the banks of the St. Marys River. [73] Fort St. Marys was another of the forts that had been built by General "Mad" Anthony Wayne in 1795 and was the northernmost fort on General Wayne's water-based supply route. Military supplies were transferred from wagons to boats at the fort and shipped to Fort Wayne in seven days. The Fort was abandoned in 1796, but still contained a blockhouse and served as a large supply depot.[74]

General Harrison left St. Marys on 24 September to visit the rest of Colonel Joshua Barbee's Regiment which was still at Fort Piqua. Captain Taul's Company continued to guard the public stores at St. Marys 25-27 September and the rest of Colonel Joshua Barbee's Regiment arrived at St. Marys from Fort Piqua on 27 September.[75]

General Harrison returned to St. Marys on the 28th and two days later, Colonel Barbee's Regiment marched a mile into the great prairie with thick grass 5'- 6' tall and performed drills until General Harrison received an urgent message from Brigadier General James Winchester near the site of Fort Defiance [76] which had been built by General "Mad" Anthony Wayne in August 1794 at the confluence of the Auglaize and Maumee Rivers. Although the fort was one of the strongest forts built in that period, it was abandoned in 1796.[77]

General Winchester told General Harrison that it appeared that he was going to be attacked near Fort Defiance by a force of 2,000-3,000 British soldiers and their Indian allies. Colonel Barbee's and Poage's Regiments were ordered to immediately march to Fort Defiance and help defend it against the anticipated attack by the British and Indians. The regiments drew several days rations of meat and flour, left St.

Marys an hour before dark on 30 September, and marched about six miles along the road to the fort before stopping to camp for the night. [78] Benjamin Jones had enlisted with the Kentucky militia to fight the British and their Indian allies and was excited that the opportunity to do that had finally arrived.

Dawn broke the next day–1 October– with the promise of rain–a promise that was soon fulfilled. The skies began to darken as the two Regiments of some 3,000 militiamen left camp as soon as it was light. Storm clouds moved in, rain began to fall around 8:00 a.m., and it rained hard all day long. The regiments marched some 24 miles towards Fort Defiance through the rain and mud before another message was received from General Winchester informing General Harrison that the British and their Indian allies had retreated down the river from Fort Defiance and were no longer threatening the Fort. [79] Benjamin Jones must have been disappointed to learn that his dream of meeting the British and their Indian allies in battle would not come true at Fort Defiance.

It continued to rain all night long and the two Regiments camped without tents on the cold, wet ground near the Oglaves River at a block house being built by the Second Regiment of Kentucky Militia commanded by Lt. Colonel William Jennings. [80] General William Harrison had ordered Colonel Jennings on 21 September to cut a road from St. Marys to a point midway between St. Marys and Fort Defiance and build a fort by the Auglaize River as a forward supply and observation post. [81] The fort included a blockhouse and a breastwork of logs covering an acre and was named for Colonel Jennings. [82]

Colonel Jennings finished construction of the fort on 2 October and Colonels Barbee's and Poage's Regiments received orders from General Harrison to cut a road from Fort Jennings some thirty miles to Fort Defiance. The rain stopped and the militiamen spent the day at Fort Jennings cleaning their guns and drying their clothes and ammunition that had been badly soaked by the rain throughout the previous day and the night just ended. The two regiments began cutting the road to Fort Defiance the next day while guarding cattle and had progressed some three miles before they were ordered by General Harrison to return to St. Marys and guard that post until further orders were received. The regiments ceased cutting the road to Fort Defiance and marched some seven miles towards St Marys before camping that night along the banks of the Oglaves River.[83]

Colonel Barbee's Regiment left its camp on the Oglaves River early in the morning on 4 October, marched some 23 miles, arrived at St. Marys midafternoon, and learned that the Indians were again around Fort Wayne. Scouts would be sent out from Taul's Company over the next couple of weeks to search for Indians near St. Marys, but none would be found. [84]

The weather was cold and rainy on the 5th and Barbee's Regiment was busy improving its camp at St. Marys and guarding cattle and the public stores for the next couple of days. News reached their camp on 8 October that the Indians had attacked and wounded several soldiers near Fort Wayne, Fort Jennings, and Fort Defiance. The entire camp was on high alert and five members of Taul's Company were sent some nine miles to the northwest of St. Marys to search for Indians, but none were found. It is not known to what extent Benjamin Jones might have participated in this or subsequent scouts. More reports about Indian attacks reached camp on 10-11 October and more soldiers of Taul's Company were sent out to scout the area for Indians, but none were found. [85]

Colonel Barbee's Regiment was still working on the stockade on the four acres around Fort St. Marys on 12-15 October and scouting details were sent out again on 14-15 October to search the adjacent country for Indians, but none were found. The Regiment finished building the stockade on the 16[th.] Although it was named Fort Barbee, many would refer to the new Fort as 'Fort St. Marys'.

Colonel Barbee ordered Micah Taul on 16 October to escort a large convoy of supplies to Fort Jennings and return immediately to

St. Marys. Sixty men from Taul's Company were assigned to guard the wagons and pack mules bound for Fort Jennings, but is not known if Benjamin Jones was one of the soldiers escorting the convoy.[86]

Two of Barbee's companies had previously escorted a convoy of supplies to Fort Jennings and had not returned. It was feared that they might have been killed or captured by Indians, but it was later learned that Colonel Jennings had detained the companies at the Fort. It took three days for the convoy guarded by Taul and his men to reach Fort Jennings and it arrived safely without any problems from the Indians. Colonel Jennings wanted to prevent Taul and his men from returning to St. Marys, but Taul refused to remain at the Fort. He and his men drew two days rations of beef and flour and left early the next morning against the protest and orders of Colonel Jennings who threatened to detain them by force. The other two companies that had been detained by General Jennings returned to St. Marys with Taul. Colonel Jennings threatened to court-marshal Taul for refusing to obey his orders to remain at the fort, but nothing came of it. [87]

The Kentucky militiamen were discouraged to learn that U. S. forces stationed at Lewiston, New York has been defeated at the Battle of Queenston Heights near Queenston in Upper Canada on 13 October 1812. The American forces commanded by Major General Stephen Van Rensselaer had attempted to cross the Niagara River to establish a foothold in Canada on the Canadian River before the arrival of winter, but the Americans were unable to get most of their forces across the river before British reinforcements arrived and forced them to surrender. [88] It was another important victory for the British, but for the Americans, it was the second defeat in a series of four invasions planned at the beginning of the war to seize Canadian territory and force Great Britain to negotiate a peace favorable to the U. S.

The news circulating in camp was not all bad. The U.S. Navy frigate *USS United States*, commanded by Stephan Decatur, had defeated the *HMS Macedonian* on 25 October 1812 in the eastern

Atlantic–a long way from any American port. The battle began with a long-range artillery duel between the two ships and the *Macedonian* was seriously damaged and forced to surrender. It was the second victory of the war in a clash between single frigates of the British and U.S. Navies and was a notable achievement for the Americans.[89]

Colonel Barbee's Regiment spent a cold and uneventful winter with snow two feet deep within the stockade it built at St. Marys. Captain Taul later wrote that "nothing very material occurred at our post during the winter. We had the same unpleasant, uninteresting round of escorting convoys of provisions to the troops in advance of us, particularly Fort Wayne, Fort Jennings, Fort Defiance." [90]

It may have been an uneventful winter for Tual's Company at St. Marys, but it wasn't uneventful, immaterial, or uninteresting for the *USS Constitution* which engaged the *HMS Java* in a three-hour single-ship battle outside Portuguese territorial waters on 29 December 1812. The *USS Constitution*, commanded by Captain William Bainbridge, had sailed with the *USS Hornet*, commanded by Captain James Lawrence, from Boston on 13 December 1812. The two ships arrived off the coast of Brazil on 26 December and the *USS Hornet* was sent to port at St. Salvador while the *USS Constitution* continued to sail off the Portugal Coast in search of British ships. On 29 December, Captain Bainbridge spotted the *HMS Java* which began chasing the *Constitution* and the two ships prepared for battle.[91]

The fighting began at 2:00 p.m. on the 29th with a long-range artillery duel and the two ships closed to within half a mile of each other. The *Constitution* opened fire with a broadside that accomplished nothing. The two ships then began to exchange broadsides at close range and the *Constitution's* wheel controlling its rudder was shot away. The *Java* lost a mast with its rigging collapsing to her deck. The ships separated and worked to repair their damage. The *Constitution* returned an hour later and closed on the *Java* before her damage could be repaired. The *Java* was unable to defend herself and surrendered. The *Java* had taken so much damage that she was not worth taking as a prize and was set on fire, exploded, and sunk on New Year's Day.[92]

It was another great victory against a British frigate for the *USS Constitution* and Captain Bainbridge joined Captain Isaac Hull as a U.S. Naval hero. The Royal Navy was shocked that it had lost three consecutive clashes between single frigates of the two navies within six months-the *USS Constitution* and the *HMS Guerriere* on 19 August 1812, the *USS United States* and the *HMS Macedonian* on 25 October 1812, and the *USS Constitution and the HMS Java* on 29 December 1812–and the British Admiralty changed its rules of engagement in July 1813 to prohibit their captains from fighting single-ship battles with American frigates.[93]

The year 1812 drew to a close and was an inauspicious beginning to America's war with Great Britain despite America's demonstrated ability to effectively fight one-on-one ship battles against the world's greatest Navy. The Canadians had not embraced General William Hull's invasion; Fort Michilimackinac on the Straits of Mackinac between Lake Michigan and Lake Huron had been captured; Fort Dearborn had been evacuated with half of the garrison, women, and children massacred; Fort Amherstburg, Britain's only garrison on the Detroit River, had not been captured; the Americans lost the Battle of Queenston Heights on the Niagara River; Fort Detroit had been surrendered to the British with the surrounding village and the entire Army of the Northwest; the Michigan Territory had come under British control; and Indian hostilities continued throughout the Territory.

The new year began much like the old year had ended. Word was received in Taul's camp that the United States suffered a devastating defeat in a series of battles with the British and their Indian allies on 18-23 January 1813 during an effort to retake Fort Detroit. Winter had come with its frozen rivers and lake shores and General Harrison was finally able to move his army north. He divided his army of 6,500 men into three columns, commanded by General James Winchester,

General Simon Perkins, and Brigadier General Edward Tupper and planned to march them separately to the Maumee River rapids then march together to Fort Detroit.[94]

On 20 December, Harrison had ordered General Winchester to march his column to the rapids. Winchester's column of some 1,200 men marched through a deep snow and reached the rapids on 10 January and began building a fortified camp on the north bank of the Maumee River some thirty-five miles northeast of the small American village of Frenchtown on the River Raisin. After Fort Detroit has been captured by the British, the Frenchtown militia surrendered and the village was now garrisoned by fifty Canadian militia and some one hundred Indians.[95]

General Winchester received several requests from the American settlers at Frenchtown to rescue them from the small garrison at the village. Although Winchester had been ordered by Harrison to remain at the rapids until the other two columns arrived then march together to Fort Detroit, Winchester decided to send a relief detachment commanded by Lt. Colonel William Lewis north to Frenchtown and that decision would prove fatal to Harrison's efforts to retake Fort Detroit. [96] Colonel Lewis led a force of some 667 Kentuckians and 100 local Michigan militiamen across the frozen Maumee River and along the frozen shore of Lake Erie to the River Raisin. He crossed the frozen River Raisin on 18 January 1813 and attacked the garrison at Frenchtown and forced the British garrison to leave. The Americans had won the battle and rescued the village, but the fight was far from over.[97]

When British Brigadier General Henry Procter, commander of the British forces around Detroit, heard that the Americans had captured Frenchtown, he marched 597 regular troops from Fort Amherstburg with some 800 Indians towards Frenchtown. Proctor's force surprised the American forces at the village before daybreak on 22 January. The Americans were attacked from three sides, retreated, and were ultimately surrounded on a narrow road. Over 200 of the

400 Americans were killed–many of which were tomahawked and scalped during the retreat. General Proctor demanded that Winchester surrender the rest of his troops, but he refused. After another three hours of fighting during which another 300 Americans were killed and an additional 500 were captured, Winchester surrendered the rest of his troops, but the fighting was still not over.[98]

On the morning of 23 January, the prisoners who could walk were marched from Frenchtown to Fort Amherstburg and the prisoners left behind were massacred by the Indians. The fighting was finally over in what would become one of the bloodiest battles of the war and General Harrison was forced to abandon his winter campaign to retake Fort Detroit. [99] News of the massacre infuriated Benjamin Jones and the other militiamen of Taul's Company. They vowed to "Remember the River Raisin" and hoped they would have an opportunity to meet the British and their Indian allies in battle before the militiamen returned to Wayne County.

More bad news was received by Taul's militiamen shortly before their term of service was to end in March. The American garrison of some 250 soldiers at the old French Fort near the village of Ogdensburg, New York was attacked and captured by the British on 22 February 1813. British Major General George MacDonald's force of 520 men crossed the frozen Saint Lawrence River with guns mounted on sleds and entered the village with little resistance. After a light skirmish in which twenty American soldiers were killed, six were wounded, and seventy were captured, the American garrison retreated and abandoned the village. It was a small, but important victory for the British because it ended the American threat to British supply lines on the upper St. Lawrence River for the rest of the war. [100]

The term of service for the men of Taul's Company was to end on 22 March 1813 and the Company was marched some 100 miles to Cincinnati, paid, and discharged. The battle with the British and their Indian allies that Benjamin Jones had so ardently sought never happened and he must have been disappointed as he headed home to

Wayne County with the rest of Taul's militiamen. The night before they arrived back home, they camped at Somerset in Pulaski County some nine miles from the Cumberland River–the county line between Wayne and Pulaski Counties. They crossed the river the next morning and were welcomed home by citizens of Wayne County gathered in large numbers at different houses along the road.[101] The militiamen were treated as heroes even though they never met the British and their Indian allies in battle.

Taul's Company arrived home on 21 March 1813–the day before the militiamen's six-month term of service was to end. The next day was county court day and Taul took a great deal of pride in talking with the families of the men who served with him during the last six months and said that "every man, who went out with me from Wayne County, returned home in good health, and in good credit." A few weeks later, the citizens of Wayne County gave a barbeque at Monticello to honor the men who served with Captain Taul's Militia Company. Taul delivered an address to those attending the barbeque and later said that he "endeavored to do justice to the worthy men who had served under me." [102] Benjamin Jones was one of those worthy men and must have been proud to have been honored for his service with Captain Taul.

Benjamin Jones' term of service with Micah Taul's Company had ended, but the war had not. It would last another twenty-three months and the Americans would be involved in a large number of significant engagements with the British before year's end.

6

WAR ON THE WATER

When the war began, the U. S. Navy was concentrated along the Atlantic coast with only four small ships on the Great Lakes and Britain gained control of the Lakes early in the war. It soon became evident to the United States that Canada could not be easily invaded by land because of non-existent and poor roads along the Canadian border-especially in Upper Canada-and the control of the Great Lakes and the St. Lawrence River would be one of the keys to the successful prosecution of the war.[103]

In September 1812, the U.S. Navy had ordered Captain Isaac Chauncy to assume command of naval forces on Lakes Erie and Ontario and gain control of the Lakes. Chauncey created a squadron of fighting ships on Lake Ontario at Sacket's Harbor, New York supported by ground troops commanded by Major General Henry Dearborn.[104] Two brigades of U.S. troops commanded by Brigadier General Zebulon Pike reinforced General Dearborn's troops at the town after a difficult winter march from Plattsburg [105] and the war on the water would accelerate with the coming of spring in 1813.

Benjamin Jones must have struggled to continue to follow the progress of the war and would eagerly seek news about the battles fought. Monticello was the County Seat of Wayne County and people from throughout the county of some 6,300 citizens would frequently visit the town for legal and other purposes. They often reported news about the war and it was welcomed and repeated regardless of how current or accurate it was. Benjamin would celebrate news about the victories won and agonize over the defeats suffered. Information was sketchy; it was often old; and at times he must have worried about the outcome of the war.

A little over a month after Benjamin returned to Wayne County, Kentucky with Micah Taul's Company, the ice on Lake Ontario had sufficiently thawed to enable a squadron of fourteen armed U.S. vessels to leave Sacket's Harbor and it did on 24 April 1813. Some 1,700 soldiers commanded by General Pike embarked from Sacketts Harbor on 24 April and sailed towards the north shore of Lake Ontario with the intent to capture York, the capitol of Upper Canada. [106]

Two days after the ships left Sackett's Harbor, another contingent of troops, commanded by British Major General Henry Proctor, left the mouth of the Maumee River on 26 April bound for Fort Meigs on the south bank of the river near the Miami rapids. A force of 533 regular British troops, 462 Canadian militiamen, and some 1,250 Indians led by Shawnee Chief Tecumseh marched up the Maumee River and besieged the Fort that had been constructed earlier that month by General William Henry Harrison. As they approached the Fort, the British and their Indian allies set up batteries along the north side of the river and began bombarding the Fort on 1 May.[107]

Four days later, a detachment of 866 U.S. troops, commanded by Colonel William Dudley, from Brigadier General Green Clay's Brigade of Kentucky militia landed from boats on the river and disabled many of the British batteries before being attacked by a large force of Indians. All but 150 of Dudley's men were killed or captured during the attack. The militiamen surviving the massacre made their way to Fort Meigs with the rest of Clay's Brigade and helped defend it until the siege was lifted by General Proctor on 9 May after most of the Indians had abandoned the British and headed back to Canada. The successful defense of Fort Meigs was a notable victory for the Americans and must have been celebrated by Benjamin Jones and the other militiamen in Taul's Company. [108]

Meanwhile, the first wave of Pike's soldiers aboard Commodore Chauncey's ships from Sackett's Harbor landed four miles west of York early in the morning on 27 April. The town was not heavily fortified and subsequent landings of American soldiers quickly led to the surrender of Fort York, the town, and dockyard. Over the next three days, the soldiers looted the town and set fire to government buildings. The attack on York did not cripple the British Navy on Lake Ontario, but it did capture ordinance and supplies bound for British vessels on Lake Erie and weakened the British squadron on that lake. [109]

Although Britain had successfully repulsed numerous American attempts to invade Canada since the war began, the defense of Canada remained a priority for the British. The American army had increased in size and capability and had deployed more U.S. soldiers along the Canadian frontier. The British decided it was necessary to shift America's attention from invading Canada to defending its own territory and initiated a blockade of the Chesapeake Bay between Maryland and Virginia. The blockade would accomplish its purpose as the British Navy wrought havoc on many of the small American ports on the Bay.[110]

British Admiral Sir John Warren had been sent to Chesapeake Bay in December 1812 and the British effectively closed the Bay to American shipping. The blockade had been strengthened in early March 1813 when Rear Admiral George Cockburn with additional ships joined Admiral Warren on the Chesapeake. Cockburn was a fighter and by mid-April, he began raiding small American towns and plantations along the Upper Chesapeake Bay and avenged the burning of York. [111]

On 29 April 1813, Cockburn attacked and burned Frenchtown, Maryland. On that same day, he attacked Elk River at the northeastern corner of the Bay, but was repulsed by the militia manning a battery that later became Fort Defiance. Cockburn then attacked and burned Havre de Grace on Maryland's western shore at the mouth of the Susquehanna River on 3 May. That same day, he burned a warehouse at Smith's Ferry and attacked the Principio Iron Works on the Northeast River–one of the most valuable Iron Works in America–and destroyed forty-six cannons which were ready to be shipped to U.S. ports to strengthen their defenses against the British navy. Two days later on 5 May, Cochran attacked and burned the towns of Fredericktown and Georgetown on the opposite banks of the Sassafras River before returning to the mouth of the Bay.[112]

While Cochran was raiding small American ports along the upper Chesapeake Bay, the Americans were preparing to attack Fort George–the westernmost British fort on Lake Ontario at the mouth of the Niagara River across the river from the American Fort Niagara. Some 4,000 U.S. soldiers commanded by General Dearborn had left York on 1 May aboard Commodore Chauncey's ships and began to bombard Fort George on 25 May from Fort Niagara, their positions along the Niagara River, and Chauncey's ships. On 27 May, American troops began landing west of the mouth of the river and advanced along the beach to the Fort and were attacked by British troops. More American troops came ashore and the British incurred heavy casualties, realized that they were significantly outnumbered, and retreated to Beaver Dams before falling back to Burlington Heights near the western end of Lake Ontario. [113]

When most of the American troops at Sacket's Harbor had left the town aboard Chauncey's ships to attack York leaving Sacket's Harbor lightly defended, Britain saw an opportunity to capture Sacket's Harbor and destroy its shipyard. British soldiers left Kingston aboard a small squadron of ships on 27 May, arrived off Sacket's Harbor early the next morning, and started to attack the town, but aborted the attack when unidentified ships appeared outside Henderson Bay. The ships were an American convoy and the British pursued and caught up with the convoy near Stoney Point on Henderson Bay. The Americans abandoned their ships and fled into the woods on Stoney Point. The fleeing Americans were pursued by the British and surrendered after a short fight.[114]

The American force at Sacket's Harbor strengthened its defenses while the British were capturing the American convoy and were prepared to defend the town when the British returned to Sacket's Harbor and resumed its attack on 29 May. The town's defenders fell back to their blockhouses and repulsed every British attempt to storm their fortifications. The British realized that they could not break through the town's defenses, retreated to the British ships, and sailed to Kingston. It was a welcome victory for the Americans who had successfully defended the base for America's naval squadron on Lake Ontario and the good news must have been celebrated by Taul's Company. [115]

The good news was followed by bad news when the United States lost its first major one-on-one ship battle with the British Navy on 1 June 1813 when the *USS Chesapeake* was captured by the *HMS Shannon* in a short, but intense battle off Boston Harbor. The two ships met some twenty miles east of Boston between Cape Ann and Cape Cod and opened fire on each other at 6:00 p.m. on 1 June while just 115 feet apart. The *Chesapeake* was heavily damaged during the intense gunnery duel, boarded by British seamen, and captured in the battle which lasted less than twenty minutes. It was a humiliating defeat for the Americans and a great victory for the British Navy. The *Shannon* towed the *Chesapeake* to Halifax, Nova Scotia and its surviving crew was imprisoned on Melville Island.[116]

The British then conducted a raid against American troops encamped at Stoney Creek on the night of 5-6 June. Some 3,500 U.S. troops, commanded by Brigadier Generals William Winder and John Chandler, were on their way to attack the British at Burlington Heights when they were surprised in a daring nighttime attack by 700 soldiers commanded by British Lieutenant John Harvey. Britain's hit-and-run raid was a success. Generals Winder and Chandler were captured with their field guns and the American troops were forced to return to Fort George. It was a great victory for the British and significantly damaged the American efforts to conquer the western part of Upper Canada.[117]

In the meantime, the Americans won a great victory against a much larger British force at the Battle of Craney Island near Norfolk and Portsmouth, Virginia on 22 June 1813. British Admiral Sir George Cockburn, still blockading Chesapeake Bay, landed some 700 Royal Marines and soldiers at Hoffler's Creek near the mouth of the Nansemond River to the west of Craney Island on 22 June to advance against the shipyard in Portsmouth, capture the *USS Constellation*, and attack Norfolk. The British were driven back and were forced to retreat to their ships, sparing Norfolk and Portsmouth from a British attack. [118]

Two days later on 24 June some 600 U.S. soldiers, commanded by Colonel Charles Boerstler. were ambushed on their way from Fort George to attack a small British outpost at Beaver Dams. The American soldiers were ambushed by some 400 Mohawk Indians in a heavily wooded area some 1.5 miles from Beaver Dams and surrendered to a small British detachment led by Lieutenant James FitzGibbon who convinced Boerstler that the Indians would slaughter the Americans if they did not surrender. The Battle of Beaver Dams along with the British raid at Stoney Creek some two weeks earlier ended American efforts to conquer the western part of Upper Canada.[119]

The day after the engagement at Beaver Dams, British forces swarmed over the undefended beach at Celey's Plantation near Hampton, Virginia, captured the town, and spent the next several days looting and burning the town and abusing its citizens in retaliation for Britain's humiliating defeat at Craney Island. The entire town was left in ruins and another battle on the water had been lost by the Americans.[120]

British Admiral George Cockburn sailed up the Chesapeake Bay after destroying Hampton, Virginia and decided to attack the shipyards at St. Michaels, Maryland. At midnight on 10 August 1813, a British force landed and attacked a battery protecting the harbor. The militia manning the battery was forced to abandon its guns and the British advanced on the town, but were repulsed by the battery protecting the town. The British retreated and the American militia won a decisive victory without a single casualty. The battle was small, but significant because it saved St. Michaels' shipyards from the British. [121]

The Americans won a larger, more significant battle in just one month on 10 September 1813 off the coast of Ohio at Put-in-Bay on Lake Erie when a U. S. Navy squadron of five schooners, three brigs, and one sloop commanded by Oliver Hazard Perry captured a British squadron of two ships, one brig, two schooners, and one sloop commanded by Robert Heriot Barclay. Commodore Perry saw Barclay's squadron heading for the American ships anchored in Put-in-Bay on the morning of 10 September. Commodore Perry's ships put out to sea and both squadrons prepared for battle. The American squadron closed on the British ships and the *HMS Detroit* fired the first shot at 11:45 a.m. The battle was intense and Perry transferred his flag to the *USS Niagara* just before the *USS Lawrence* was captured. The battle continued and *The USS Niagara* captured the *HMS Detroit* and the *HMS Queen Charlotte* around 3:00 p.m. The smaller British vessels tried to flee, but were overtaken and captured. The entire British squadron of six ships was captured and the Americans would control Lake Erie for the rest of the war.[122]

Battle on Lake Erie

Another impressive American victory occurred less than a month later on 5 October 1813 when General William Henry Harrison's force of some 3,500 infantry and cavalry defeated Shawnee Indian Chief Tecumseh's Indian Confederacy and their British allies at the Battle of the Thames near Chatham in Upper Canada. British Major General Henry Procter commanded a force of some 800 regular soldiers and chiefs Tecumseh and Roundhead led about 500 Indians in the battle that the Americans won decisively. Tecumseh and his war Chief Roundhead were killed and Tecumseh's Indian alliance collapsed. It was a great victory for the Americans and reestablished American control over the Northwest frontier. [123]

Many of the soldiers serving under General Harrison were from Kentucky–some were from Wayne County–and Benjamin Jones must have been proud to learn that the Kentuckians had fought the British and their Indian allies and won a decisive battle on the Thames River. It looked like the year 1813 would end on a positive note for the Americans, but the year was not over. Benjamin's struggle to determine information about the war would continue and he would soon learn that the Americans would lose a number of battles before year end.

The first of those battles was fought along the marshy shores of the Chateauguay River near Montreal on 25-26 October. U.S. General Wade Hampton with a force of some 3,000 troops set out to invade Lower Canada and capture Montreal, but his campaign ran into trouble before he crossed the border. Some 1,000 of his soldiers from the New York militia refused to cross the Canadian border and General Hampton began his attempt to capture Montreal with a weakened army. [124]

The Canadian force at Montreal was entrenched behind well-built defensive works and U.S. Colonel Robert Purdy led a force of some 1,500 men on 25 October to gain a position behind the Canadian defenses, but became lost in the woods and was unable to take a flanking position against the Canadians and their Indian allies. Early the next morning, U.S. General George Izard began a frontal assault on the Canadian position without the advantage of Purdy's troops attacking the Canadian's flanks. The assault lasted several hours with intense thrusts and counter thrusts by both sides. By 3:00 p.m. that afternoon, Hampton recognized that his attack would fail and ordered his men to withdraw. The Americans lost 23 killed, 33 wounded, and 29 missing in the battle at Chateauguay and lost an opportunity to capture Montreal.[125]

Two weeks later on 11 November, the Americans lost another battle along the shores of the St. Lawrence River–the battle of Crysler's farm–in the middle of a farmer's field between Morrisburg and Cornwall. A flotilla of well-armed American ships commanded by General James Wilkinson descended the St. Lawrence River to combine forces with General Wade Hampton and attack Montreal. General Wilkinson remained with his ship and Brigadier General John Parker Boyd with 2,500 infantry troops marched to meet the forces of General Wade Hampton who had just lost the Battle at Chateauguay River. Boyd had been persistently pursued by a British force of some 2,000 soldiers, commanded by Lieutenant Colonel Joseph Morrison, and their Indian allies. Boyd tired of being pursued and decided to confront the British. He set up headquarters at a local tavern on 10 November with the British soldiers encamped just two miles away at the farm of loyalist John Crysler. [126]

The British and their Indian allies attacked General Boyd's position the next morning, but were initially driven back. Their efforts were supported by a small flotilla of gunboats on the St. Lawrence River and they eventually wore the Americans down. Boyd realized that he was beaten, called a retreat, and moved his troops to French Mills for the winter. Boyd lost 340 killed and wounded with 100 captured at Crysler's Farm and it was a terrible defeat for the Americans that ended their attempt to capture Montreal. [127]

The American garrison of some 200 soldiers at Fort George, commanded by Brigadier General George McClure, abandoned Fort George on 10 December, burned the village of Newark, and moved to Fort Niagara on the American side of the river where it empties into Lake Ontario. Nine days later during the night of 18 December, a force of 500 British soldiers, 50 Canadian militiamen and 12 Indians, commanded by Colonel John Murray, crossed the Niagara River some three miles above Fort Niagara, captured American pickets in the village of Youngstown, and advanced to the Fort. The garrison was surprised by the night attack and was easily captured the next day.[128]

The fall of Fort Niagara enabled the British, Canadians, and Indians to ravage the countryside on the American side of the river. They destroyed Fort Schlosser near Niagara Falls and the villages of Youngstown, Black Rock, Lewiston, Manchester, and Tuscarora before capturing the American forces at the Battle of Buffalo on 30 December 1813. The navy yard on Buffalo Creek was destroyed with three armed schooners and one sloop and all but four of Buffalo's buildings were burned. [129] The year had ended with America's militias routed, ships destroyed, towns and supplies burned, and civilians brutalized and killed. [130] It was a terrible ending to the year and Benjamin Jones and most other Americans didn't know what to expect during the year 1814 that was about to begin.

In 1811, Shawnee Chief Tecumseh had travelled south to the Mississippi Territory and tried to convince the Southern Indian Tribes to join his Confederacy of Northern Tribes in their struggle against white settlers who continually encroached on their ancestral lands. He returned in 1812 to explain how the Northern Indians had become allies of the British in their war against the Americans and had driven the Americans out of Detroit and the Michigan Territory. He promised that the British and Spanish in Florida would support the Southern Indians' fight against the Americans. [131]

Some of the Cherokees sided with the United States and the Chickasaws and Choctaws were not interested in war with the Americans, but many of the Creeks were hostile towards the Americans and two factions developed within the Creek Nation–the

Red Sticks were followers of Tecumseh and welcomed a war against the Americans while the remainder of the Creek Nation sought to adopt the white culture. War broke out between the two factions in the later part of 1813 and the American struggle with the British would extend into the Creek Indian Nation, Spanish-controlled Florida, and along the Gulf Coast in the South. [132]

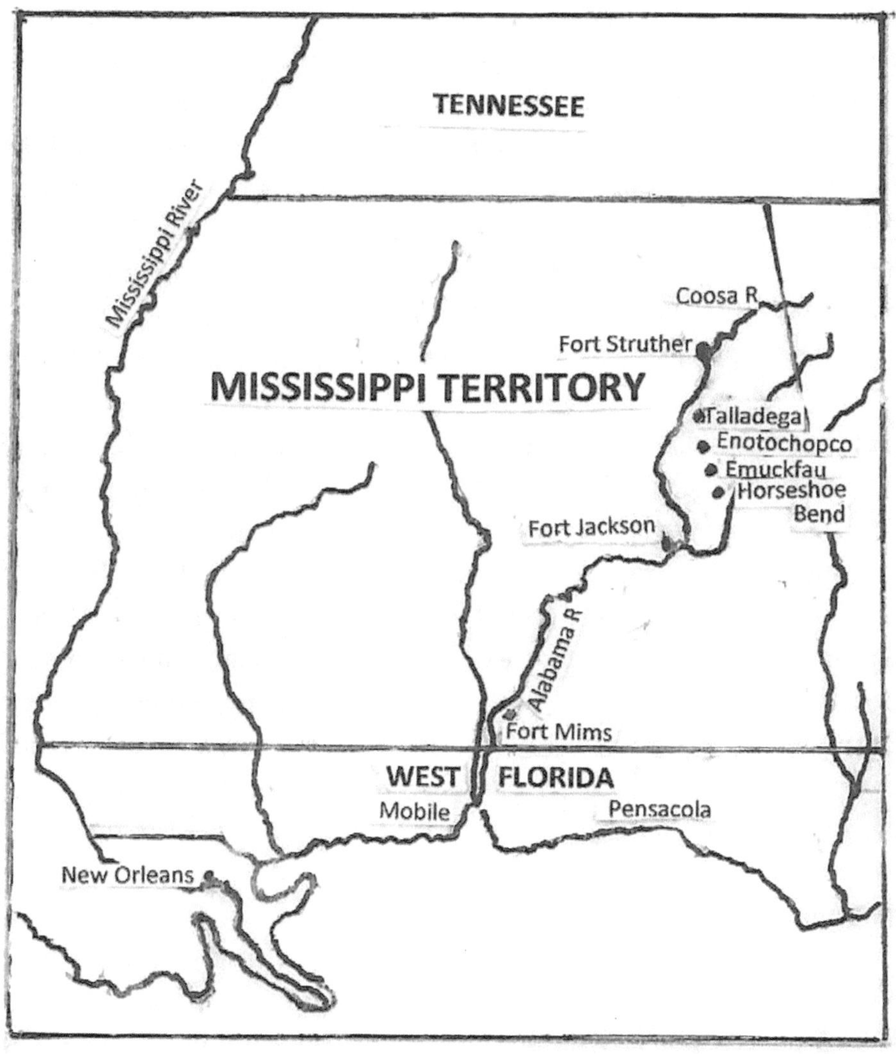

The Southern Frontier

On 30 August 1813, a force of some 700 Red Stick warriors had attacked and destroyed Fort Mims in the Tensaw District of the Mississippi Territory. Some 250 of the Fort's defenders were killed and 100 were captured during the fight and civilian men, women, and children were massacred after the battle. It was a great victory for the Red Stick warriors and prompted U.S. military action against the Creek Nation. [133]

When news of the massacre at Fort Mims reached Andrew Jackson, who had been appointed Major General of the Tennessee Militia in 1802, he called for volunteers to rendezvous at Fayette, Tennessee on 4 October 1813 and march into the Mississippi Territory and end the Red Stick Creek Indian menace. Among those who assembled with Jackson at Fayette, Tennessee and fought with him in the Mississippi Territory were Davy Crockett and Sam Houston and the three men were destined to become major American historical figures. [134]

Andrew Jackson would become a national hero after the Battle of New Orleans, would serve as the first governor of the Florida Territory, would serve in the U.S. House of Representatives and the U.S. Senate before becoming the 7th President of the United States in 1829. [135] Davy Crockett would become a folk hero as a frontiersman, soldier and politician who would represent Tennessee in the U.S. House of Representatives and take part in the Texas Revolution against Mexico, fighting and dying in the Battle of the Alamo. [136] Sam Houston would be seriously wounded in the Battle of Horseshoe Bend, would represent Tennessee in the U.S. House of Representatives and become Governor of Tennessee. He would play a major role in the Texas Revolution against Mexico. He helped organize the provisional government of Texas and the Texas Independence Convention of 1836. He would be appointed Commander-in-Chief of the militia units that constituted the Texas Army and would defeat Santa Anna's Army at the Battle of San Jacinto which won Texas' independence from Mexico. He later became the President of Texas and was instrumental in getting Texas annexed to the United States. He would serve as Governor of Texas, a U.S. Senator, and an unsuccessful U.S. presidential candidate in the presidential elections of 1856 and 1860. [137]

Jackson's army left Tennessee before the end of the October, reached Ten Islands in the Mississippi Territory on 1 November, and immediately began building Fort Strother on the upper Coosa River. The stockade fort was built on a bluff of the river and would become Jackson's supply base to attack the Red Stick warriors. It was rectangular in shape with blockhouses at each corner and included eight hospital huts, twenty-five tents, and a supply building. [138]

Before the construction of Fort Strother was completed, Jackson received a request for help from friendly Creek Indians who were being besieged by Red Stick warriors at Fort Leslie–a small palisade built around Leslie's trading post. Jackson left a contingent of soldiers to guard Fort Strothers, arrived outside Fort Leslie on 9 November and attacked and drove the Red Stick Indians from the field with casualties of 300 killed and 110 wounded in what became known as the Battle of Talladega. There was a lull in the fighting between Jackson's army and the Red Stick warriors after the battle and Jackson's army returned to Fort Strother and would spend the winter at the Fort. [139]

On 29 November 1813, a Georgia militia company of some 900 soldiers and 450 allied Creek Indians, commanded by General John Floyd, surrounded and stormed the Creek village of Autossee, killing some 200 Red Stick warriors and burning Autossee and the nearby village of Tallasee to the ground. [140] The Battles at Fort Mims, Talladega, and Autossee were a preview of the fighting that would occur in the Mississippi Territory during 1814.

7

1814

The war on the water would continue in 1814 as the British launched another series of raids along the Chesapeake Bay. Rear Admiral George Cockburn and Major General Robert Ross would fight another eighteen battles before their Chesapeake Campaign ended with the Battle of Fort McHenry in September. [141] But the first significant conflict in the new year was not on the Chesapeake Bay; it was not in Canada or along the Canadian border; and it was not with the British or the Canadians. It was with the Red Stick Creek Indian warriors at the Horseshoe Bend of the Tallapoosa River in the Mississippi Territory.

Jackson's army had dwindled in size over the winter due to desertions and the expiration of enlistments and he decided to combine his force with a Georgia militia. While on the way to meet the militia, Jackson's force was attacked by Red Stick warriors on 22-24 January 1814 in the Battles of Emuckfow and Enotachopo Creek. The militiamen repulsed the attackers, but were outnumbered by the Indians and forced to withdraw to Fort Strother while the Indians continued their savage attacks on settlers on the frontier.[142]

Jackson's militia built Fort Williams in March 1814 and left the Fort in the Spring to cut its way through the forests to within six miles of the Red Sticks' camp Tehopeka near the Horseshoe Bend of the Tallapoosa River. On 27 March, General Jackson surrounded and attacked the Red Sticks with 2,600 American soldiers and 600 allied

Cherokee, Choctaw, and Lower Creek Indians. The battle lasted more than five hours and 800 of the 1,000 Red Stick warriors were killed. Chief Menawa fled with the surviving Red Stick warriors to Spanish Florida, became allies with the Seminole tribe, and would meet Jackson again at the Battle of Pensacola in the Fall.[143]

Benjamin heard little about the fighting with the Creek Indians in the Mississippi Territory, but would soon learn that the war in Europe between Britain and France had ended and Britain would send large numbers of ships, troops, war materiel, and supplies to America. He feared that the war might take a turn for the worse and it would.

In April 1814, Great Britain and its European allies proclaimed that Napoleon was the sole obstacle to the restoration of peace in Europe. Napoleon was forced to renounce his thrones in France and Italy on 11 April 1814 and was exiled to the Mediterranean Island of Elba, effectively ending Britain's war with France. [144] Britain began repealing its policies of trade restrictions and its full attention was focused on the war with its former colonies in North America. Britain began shifting more of its military resources to that war and that didn't bode well for the Americans. Albert Gallatin, Secretary of the U.S. Treasury, said "we should have to fight hereafter not for free Trade and sailors' rights, not for the Conquest of the Canadas, but for our national existence." [145]

Secretary Gallatin was right. The British were coming! America had significantly weakened its new adversary–the Red Stick Creek Indians in the Mississippi Territory–but its old adversary Great Britain was about to be strengthened.

U.S. Secretary of War John Armstrong, Jr. knew that British reinforcements were coming from Europe and he wanted to invade Canada and win a victory before they arrived. He ordered U.S. Major General Jacob Brown to capture Fort Erie opposite Buffalo.[146] Brown and his 4,500-man force crossed the Niagara River into Upper Canada at the small neck between Lakes Ontario and Erie on 3 July 1814 and moved south towards Fort Erie at the head of the Niagara River near its source in Lake Erie. The Americans attacked British pickets and demanded that the Fort with its 137-man garrison be surrendered and it was at 6:00 p.m. [147] The Americans had won an important victory and accomplished it with less than 10 casualties. Fort Erie became General Brown's new base of operations for his advance up the Niagara River and he marched his forces up the Niagara River and fought the British two days later near the town of Chippawa. [148]

Early on 5 July, British forces, commanded by Major General Phineas Riall, crossed the Chippawa River and engaged two brigades commanded by Brigadier Generals Winfield Scott and Peter Porter in a field between Street's Creek and the Chippawa River. The lines of the two sides advanced to within 100 yards of each other and exchanged fire for some 25 minutes before the British fell back with heavy loses and retreated to the north side of the Chippawa River. The Americans had won another victory and two days after the battle, General Brown and his forces crossed the Chippawa River upstream from Riall's forces and forced them to fall back to Fort George.[149] The Americans then marched northward and burned the settlement of St. David's on 12 July before returning to Chippawa on 24 July to resupply their army.[150]

The British had been monitoring the movements of Brown's army since the Battle of Chippawa and General Riall advanced to Lundy's Lane to keep a closer eye on the Americans who had returned to the Chippawa River. On 25 July, General Riall was reinforced by 1,700 troops from Fort George commanded by British Lieutenant Governor Gordon Drummond who took command of the British forces and ordered them to advance towards Brown's soldiers who had left Chippawa and moved north. The British encountered Brigadier General Winfield Scott's brigade of over 1,000 soldiers when it emerged from a forest around 6:00 p.m. into a field in front of a British artillery position about one mile west of Niagara Falls. Scott's forces came under severe fire and by nightfall had suffered heavy casualties before they were relieved by two brigades commanded by Brigadier Generals

Eleazer W. Ripley and Peter B. Porter. Their brigades captured the British guns and repulsed several British attempts to recover the guns.[151] The battle at Lundy's Lane was fierce with a lot of fighting at close quarters. Casualties numbered 1,731 in the battle which would become one of the bloodiest battles of the entire war. The British incurred 878 casualties with 84 killed and the Americans suffered 853 casualties with 174 killed. The fighting finally ended around midnight with both sides too exhausted to continue to fight. Neither side won a decisive victory, but the American advance into Upper Canada had been stopped and the Americans withdrew to Fort Erie the next day. General Brown abandoned his campaign to invade Upper Canada and the balance of power on the Niagara Peninsula shifted from the Americans to the British.[152]

When Benjamin Jones learned that representatives of Great Britain and the United States had met in Ghent, United Netherlands on 8 August 1814 to negotiate an end to the war, he must have been pleased that the war was about to end. He might have thought about his service with the Kentucky militia and regretted again that he never had an opportunity to fight the British and their Indian allies before the war ended, but the war was not about to end.

The British began the peace negotiations by demanding that an Indian barrier state supported by the British be created in the American Northwest Territory; they demanded that the Americans be prohibited from having any naval force on the Great Lakes; and they demanded that the British have certain transit rights on the Mississippi River. The demands were totally unacceptable to the Americans; the negotiations broke down; and the war continued. [153] No one knew for certain how uncertain the future was. With the war ended in Europe, Britain had the ability to significantly increase the size of its army and navy in America and could more aggressively prosecute the war in 1814 and it would.

The day after peace negotiations began in Ghent, General Andrew Jackson forced the Creek Indians to sign the Treaty of Fort Jackson on 9 August. The Creeks ceded 23 million acres of their territory to the United States and the Creek Indian War had ended, but fighting with the Red Stick Creek Indians and their British allies had not. Chief Menawa fled with some 200 surviving Red Stick warriors to Florida and would meet General Jackson again at the Battle of Pensacola in the Fall. [154]

Meanwhile, four British warships, commanded by Sir Thomas Masterman Hardy, arrived offshore at Stonington, Connecticut on 9 August and bombarded the village for four days. The ships inflicted considerable damage to the village, but the two guns defending the village inflicted more damage to the British ships and forced them to withdraw on 12 August.[155] The village had been successfully defended, but the British would attack another village in twelve days and the results would be drastically different.

The end of their war with France enabled Britain to begin moving large numbers of troops across the Atlantic to America. Major-General Robert Ross, a veteran officer in Britain's war with France, was transferred to America from the southwestern part of France with some 3,000 troops in August 1814 and reported to Vice Admiral Sir Alexander Cochran in Bermuda. Ross's troops increased the size of Cochran's army to more than 4,000 soldiers and Cochran sailed his army from Bermuda to support the forces of Rear-Admiral Sir George Cockburn on Chesapeake Bay.[156]

Vice Admiral Cochran and Rear-Admiral Cockburn decided to attack a fleet of American gunboats that had taken refuge from the British Navy in the Patuxent River east of Washington. General Ross's army was landed near the mouth of the Patuxent River at Benedict, Maryland on 19 August 1814 just seven days after the British raid on Stonington, Connecticut had ended. [157] Ross marched his troops up the river to capture the American gunboats commanded by Commodore Joshua Barney, but Barney destroyed fifteen of the gunboats to keep them from being captured by the British before retreating to the village of Bladensburg on the road to Washington.

Ross's army attacked Bladensburg on 24 August. The American position on the western bank of the East Branch River was strong and well defended by Barney's 400 sailors, 1,450 local militia, 420 regular soldiers, and some 5,000 additional militiamen, but when Ross attacked, the militiamen only fought briefly before fleeing the field and the battle quickly turned into a British victory. The British victory at Bladensburg left Washington vulnerable to attack and later that day Ross' troops entered Washington and burned the Executive Mansion, the U.S. Capitol, the Treasury, and the War Office before returning to their ships the next day.[158]

U.S. Capitol Burned By The British

Three days later on 27 August 1814, a British naval squadron, commanded by Commodore James Alexander Gordon, approached Fort Warburton–popularly called Fort Washington–at Digges Point on the Potomac River. The British fleet anchored near the fort and began firing. After the fort had been bombarded for some two hours,

Captain Samuel Dyson blew up the fort and its magazine of some 3,000 pounds of cannon powder shortly after 7:00 p.m. He had been ordered earlier to "advance a guard up to the main road . . . leading to the fort, and in the event of his being taken in the rear of the fort by the enemy, to blow up the fort and retire across the river." Captain Dyson did exactly that and his fifty-six-man garrison retreated after blowing up the fort. He was later court-marshaled for abandoning his post and destroying government property and was dismissed from the service. [159]

Early the next morning–28 August–the British fleet completed its destruction of Fort Washington and sailed upriver to Alexander and anchored off the town's shore. The town Council agreed to surrender the town on 29 August with 22 merchant ships and a large quantity of merchandise to avoid being bombarded by the British ships. The British occupied and plundered the town for three days before returning to the main British fleet commanded by Vice Admiral Alexander Cochrane on the Chesapeake.[160]

August had been a devastating month for the Americans. After successfully defending Stonington, Connecticut which was severely damaged by British ships, the Americans were defeated in one battle after another–at Bladensburg, Maryland, Washington, D.C., Fort Warburton near the Capitol City, and Alexandria, Virginia. The bad news jolted Benjamin and he feared that America could lose The Second War of America's Independence.

As the calendar reached September 1814, the U.S. war effort was faltering on all fronts. Britain had sent a large quantity of ships, troops, materiel, and supplies across the Atlantic and was more aggressively pursuing the war with its former colonies. The British were on the offensive and the war along the Canadian border was escalating. British General George Prevost received reinforcements of some 13,000 troops and on August's last day, crossed the Canadian border, entered the State of New York, and advanced towards Plattsburg with plans to capture the town and the entire Champlain

Valley. It appeared that the British were about to achieve another decisive victory over the struggling Americans, but appearances can be deceiving and they were. General Prevost's troops encountered and skirmished with American forces outside Plattsburg while a British Navy squadron, commanded by Captain George Downie, engaged a small American naval force, commanded by Master Commandant Thomas Macdonough, on Lake Champlain in upstate New York. Provost chose to await the results of Downie's battle with Macdonough before advancing on Plattsburgh. [161]

Commandant Macdonough decided to fight a stationary battle with the British fleet and ordered his four ships–*Eagle*, *Saratoga*, *Preble*, and *Ticonderoga*–and ten gunboats to anchor in Cumberland Bay and wait for the British squadron to come into range of his guns. They did and all ships of both fleets became engaged at close range at 9:45 a.m. on 11 September 1814. The battle raged on Lake Champlain for some two hours and the flagships of both navies–the *USS Saratoga* and the *HMS Confiance* were heavily damaged. Macdonough managed to rotate his ship and his undamaged guns blasted the *Confiance*, shattered its hull, and killed or wounded some 150 sailors. The *Confiance* had no option but to surrender and it did along with the rest of the British fleet. When General Prevost learned that the British fleet had been defeated on Lake Champlain, he called off the land battle and retreated back to Canada. [162] The Americans had won another great victory over the world's greatest navy, but it hadn't seen the last of the army commanded by British Major General Robert Ross.

Rear Admiral George Cockburn landed General Ross' army of some 5,000 men at North Point just fourteen miles from Baltimore, Maryland on the same day–11 September 1814–that the British squadron was defeated on Lake Champlain. Ross marched his army towards Baltimore and engaged the Baltimore militia commanded by Major General Samuel Smith. General Smith ordered Brigadier General John Stricker to confront the advancing British with his

3rd Brigade and he did on 12 September between Bear Creek and Bread and Cheese Creek. Ross was shot in the chest by a sniper's bullet and died soon after the battle began. Colonel Arthur Brooke took command of Ross' army and forced the Americans to retreat to Baltimore after an intense hour-long battle, but Brooke chose to wait until the British Navy had attacked and subdued Fort McHenry before he pursued the retreating Americans. [163]

The Americans had assembled some 10,000 men and 100 cannon along the Philadelphia Road to block the British advance towards Baltimore and the British Navy planned to reduce Fort McHenry to enable the navy to support the land attack against Baltimore. British warships, commanded by Vice Admiral Alexander Cochrane, began exchanging fire with Fort McHenry's cannons on 13 September, but soon withdrew out of the cannons' range and began bombing the Fort. British warships bombarded the Fort for twenty-seven straight hours with more than 1,500 cannonballs, shells, and rockets and many felt that the Fort would fall during the night, but the dawn's early light on 14 September revealed that the American flag was still there. The British bombardment of Fort McHenry had failed and there would be no naval support for Colonel Arthur Brooke's planned land assault against Baltimore. Brooke abandoned his assault against Baltimore, returned to the British ships, and sailed for New Orleans. It was a great victory for the Americans and must have influenced the peace agreement with Great Britain that would be reached before the end of the year. [164]

No major battles were fought between the British and the U.S. in October, but two notable battles occurred in November–the first in Canada and the second in Spanish Florida. The Americans won them both. The first battle was the last battle fought in Canada during the war. U.S. Brigadier General Duncan McArthur left Detroit in October 1814 on an extended raid into Canada. His force of some 700 mounted militiamen advanced into Canada and raided settlements in the Thames Valley which supplied flour and bread to British and

Canadian forces. On 30 October, McArthur's force overwhelmed the British post at Delaware and on 4 November scattered a small Canadian militia force at Oakland and ransacked the village. On 6 November, McArthur's force defeated 550 Canadian militia at Malcolm's Mills and destroyed the local mills and stores of grain. He then rode westward and captured small militia units and burned mills at Savareen Mills and Dover before discontinuing his raid on 10 November and returning to Detroit. The battle at Malcolm's Mill would be the last land battle fought in Upper Canada during the war and the British would be unable to mount any offensive against Detroit during the rest of the war because the region had been stripped of resources to support an army.[165]

The last notable battle fought in November was the first battle fought in Spanish Florida during the war. On 6 November, General Andrew Jackson led his 4,000-man army against the British and Spanish forces defending the city of Pensacola with their Creek Indian and slave allies. By 9 November, the British and their Indian allies abandoned the city along with a British naval squadron and the Spanish surrendered the city. Jackson left Pensacola to the Spanish and marched to Mobile, Alabama. While there, he received several requests to go to New Orleans and help defend that city against the British and he would. [166]

8

THE WAR FINALLY ENDS

After months of negotiations with both sides of the war experiencing more victories and defeats, Britain and the United States had tired of the war and both nations wanted peace. The peace delegates reconvened at Ghent on 1 December 1814 and signed the peace agreement a little over three weeks later on 24 December 1814, but it did not end the war. The agreement had to be formally ratified by the two governments. The treaty was approved by the British Parliament on 30 December, but news of the treaty was slow to reach the United States. The U.S. would not approve the treaty until February 1815 and in the meantime fighting between the two belligerents continued. [167]

The United States won its greatest battlefield victory of the war on 8 January 1815 when it defeated Britain's effort to capture the American port at New Orleans. Major General Andrew Jackson left Mobile, Alabama on 22 November, reached New Orleans on 1 December, and assembled an army of some 5,700 men to stop an anticipated British invasion. Rear Admiral George Cochran's British fleet arrived at Ship Island some sixty miles east of New Orleans on 8 December and landed British infantrymen below New Orleans on 23 December. General Jackson attacked the British camp in a night-time assault and withdrew two miles north after a short fight and built a strong earthwork ¾ mile in length from the Mississippi River to a cypress swamp. [168]

General Sir Edward Pakenham moved the British army to the Chalmette Plantation on 27 December and tried unsuccessfully to breach Jackson's earthworks over the next five days. He then launched a major assault against Jackson's defensive line on 8 January 1815 and suffered 2,000 casualties in less than thirty minutes. The British army retreated to Cochran's fleet on 18 January. It was a great decisive victory for the Americans who stopped the British attempt to capture New Orleans. It lost only 62 men during the fighting while the British lost 2,034 men.[169]

The U.S. Senate finally approved the Treaty of Ghent on 16 February 1815. President Madison exchanged papers ratifying the treaty with a British diplomat in Washington on 17 February, and the next day, the war was proclaimed to be over, [170] but it wasn't. The commanders of the *USS Constitution,* the *HMS Cyane,* and the *HMS Levanat* did not know that the war had ended and the three war ships fought a battle about 100 miles east of Madeira on 20 February 1815.[171]

A storm outside of Boston Harbor in late 1814 had enabled the *USS Constitution,* commanded by Captain Charles Stewart, to slip out of the harbor and avoid detection by the British squadron blockading the harbor. The *Constitution* left Boston on a commerce-raiding cruise off Bermuda, Madeira, and the coast of Portugal before sailing back towards Madeira. Captain Stewart sighted the *HMS Cyane* and *HMS Levant* sailing south of Madeira at 1:00 p.m. on 20 February 1815 and pursued the two British ships. By 5:30 p.m., the *Constitution* had closed to within 250 yards of the British ships near Porto Praya, Cape Verde Islands. [172]

The three vessels prepared to fight and the battle began at 6:10 p.m. with the *Cyane* on *Constitution's* port quarter and the *Levant* on *Constitution's* port bow. Broadsides were exchanged for some fifteen minutes before the *Constitution* successfully maneuvered to rake both British ships in rapid succession. The *Levant* drifted out of range with battered rigging, but the *Cyane* was seriously damaged and had no option but to surrender and it did at 6:50 p.m. The *Constitution* pursued the *Levant* and the battle was renewed around 8:50 p.m. The two ships exchanged broadsides and the *Levant* was forced to surrender at 9:30 p.m.[173] The U.S. Navy had won another decisive victory over the greatest navy in the entire world!

The fighting between Great Britain and the United States finally ended in the war that was officially over two days earlier. As news of the war's end made its way to Wayne County, Kentucky, Benjamin Elliott Jones must have remembered with pride his role in that war—how he had fought with Revolutionary War Veterans and the sons of such Veterans against the British and their Indian allies–and he must have remembered that his grandfather Dawson Wade, Sr. was a Veteran of the Revolutionary War and had often shared stories with Benjamin about that war and America's fight for its independence.

Benjamin now had his own story to share. He was a Veteran of the Second War of America's Independence. He had volunteered for that war on 23 August 1812 as a Private in Captain Micah Taul's Company of Infantry, Seventh Regiment, Kentucky Militia and marched to the Indiana Territory to fight the British and their Indian allies. After Fort Detroit had fallen to the British, Taul's Company was ordered to the Northwest. In September 1813, a force of 2,000-3,000 British soldiers and their Indian allies gathered around Fort Defiance at the confluence of the Anglaize and Maumee Rivers and threatened to attack the Fort. General Harrison ordered Taul's Company to immediately leave St. Marys and march to Fort Defiance to help defend the Fort and it did.

While Taul's Company was on the way to the Fort, the British and Indians retreated down the river and no longer threatened the Fort. Although Benjamin Jones and the rest of Taul's Company did not fight the British and their Indian allies at Fort Defiance or anywhere else, they were received as heroes when they returned home to Wayne County, Kentucky. Benjamin was a Veteran of The Second War of America's Independence and would never tire of telling his story about that war for the rest of his life.

9

LEAVING WAYNE COUNTY

Some three years after the end of the Second War of America's Independence, Benjamin Elliott Jones left Wayne County, Kentucky in 1815 and migrated to the Alabama Territory with his wife Viney and their children Eliza Jane and Sylvester. Why Alabama? Before he had explored Kentucky with Daniel Boone, Benjamin's grandfather Dawson Wade, Sr. had scouted for marauding Indians in their ancestral lands in what would become the Alabama Territory on 3 March 1817. [174] Perhaps Benjamin grew up listening to his grandfather's stories about Alabama and those stories sparked his imagination and created a desire to live there some day and he did.

Benjamin left Monticello, Kentucky and migrated some 300 miles south and settled in Lawrence County, Alabama some two years after the county was formed out of the Cherokee & Chickasaw Session in 1816 [175] and was living there when Alabama became the 22nd State of the Union on 14 December 1819. He later moved to Fayette County, Alabama, and would live there for the rest of his life.

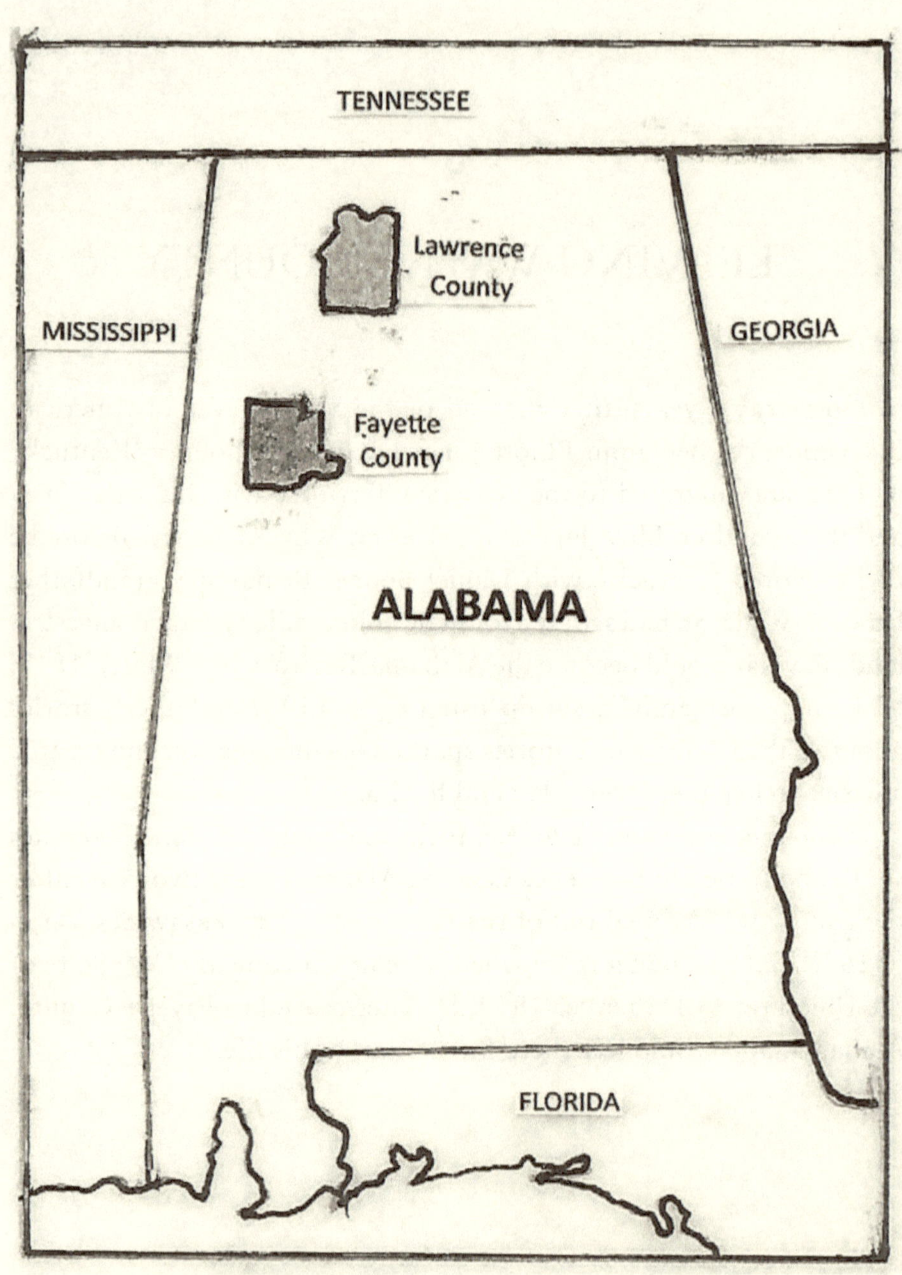

Alabama (with Lawrence & Fayette Counties shown)

Benjamin's father Rev. Elliott Jones moved to Lawrence County, Alabama in 1822 and six years later in June 1828 received an Alabama State License to perform marriages. He owned slaves and, in his will dated 25 February 1839, he bequeathed to his wife Elizabeth her "choice of two negroes." The List of Property Selected by Elizabeth Jones filed with the Probate Court in Lawrence County reflects that Elizabeth selected a Negro Woman valued at $200 and a Negro Man valued at $300. Elliott would live in Lawrence County until his death at age 77 on 16 December 1841. [176]

Benjamin's father-in-law Robert Wallace had moved from Fayette County, Kentucky to Wayne County before 1801 and lived there until his death in September 1813. Benjamin's grandfather Dawson Wade, Sr. never left Montgomery County, Kentucky and lived there until his death on 8 December 1819 in Mt. Sterling. [177]

Benjamin and Viney moved to the village of Berry in Fayette County before the birth of their daughter Frances Ann Elizabeth Jones on 9 April 1832 and Viney died there on 19 August 1840. Eight months after Viney's death, Benjamin married Narcissa Livingston on 21 April 1841. His faith was an important part of Benjamin's life and the church that first met in his home–known as The Tabernacle– became a Methodist Episcopal Church South in the 1850's. [178] The 1860 United States Federal Census reported that Benjamin's Real Estate was valued at $2,500 and his Personal Estate was valued at $9,800. [179] The 1860 United States Federal Census Slave Schedules for the East District of Fayette County, Alabama reported that Benjamin owned the ten slaves shown in Exhibit III. [180]

Benjamin successfully worked his farm in Fayette County and Schedule 4–Productions of Agriculture–of the 1860 Agricultural Census Schedule taken on 18 July 1860 by Assistant Marshal Daniel G. Kirkland preserved a record of Benjamin's farming activity for the year 1860. The schedule reported that 25 Acres of Benjamin's 400-acre farm were improved. The Cash Value of his Farm was $500 and the Value of his Farming Implements & Machinery was $65.

The Value of his Life Stock on 1 June 1860 was $425 and included 3 Horses, 5 Milch Cows, 2 Working Oxen, 5 Other Cattle, and 25 Swine. Produce during the year ending 1 June 1860 included 4 Bushels of Wheat, 300 Bushels of Indian Corn, two 400-pound Bales of Ginned Cotton, 50 Bushels of Peas & Beans, 1 lb of Cheese, and 75 lbs of Honey. The Value of Produce of Market Gardens was $50; the Value of Homemade Manufactures was $40; and the Value of Animals Slaughtered was $120. [181]

Benjamin was living in Fayette County when Alabama seceded from the Union on 11 January 1861; he was living there when the Confederate Nation was formed at Montgomery, Alabama in February; he was living there when the great War for Southern Independence began on 12 April 1861; and he saw his family experience the hardships and horrors of a Nation at war with itself.

One of Benjamin's sons–Sylvester Phipps Jones–died before the war began; another son–Elliott Priest Jones–was elected to the Alabama Secession Convention in 1861, voted against the Ordinance of Secession, refused to sign the Ordinance, and remained loyal to the Union during the conflict; [182] Benjamin's other two sons –John Wallace Jones and Robert Glass Jones–and his two sons-in-law–Richard Wesley Cole, husband of Eliza Jane, and George Shipp Gaines, husband of Frances Ann Elizabeth–fought for the Confederacy during the war.

John Wallace Jones served the Confederacy as Captain of Company K Louisiana Infantry; Robert Glass Jones served as a Private/Corporal in Company I of the 43rd Regiment Alabama Infantry; Richard Wesley Cole served as a Private of the 5th Regiment Mississippi Cavalry in General Nathan Bedford Forrest's Mississippi Cavalry Department; and George Shipp Gaines served as a Private in Captain Lafayette Newton Cole's Company B of the 8th Alabama Cavalry Regiment.

Benjamin must have struggled with his family's allegiance to both sides during the war. He had defended the United States as a militiamen in The Second War of America's Independence and must have respected and honored Elliott Priest for his efforts to prevent

Alabama from succeeding from the Union and his decision to remain loyal to the Union during the conflict, but he also must have been proud of his other two sons and his two sons-in-law who fought for the independence of the Confederacy just as his grandfather Dawson Wade, Sr. had fought in the Revolutionary War for the American colonies' independence from Great Britain.

Benjamin must have struggled to follow the progress of the War for Southern Independence just as he had struggled to follow the progress of America's Second War of Independence and must have looked forward to welcoming his family's soldiers home after the war, but he did not live to welcome them home because he died at age 73 on 19 January 1863 some 15 months before his son-in-law Richard Wesley Cole would be killed at the Battle of Fort Pillow in Lauderdale County, Tennessee on 12 April 1864 and some 27 months before General Robert E. Lee would formally surrender his Army of Northern Virginia on 12 April 1865 at the village of Appomattox Court House, Virginia.

Benjamin must have anticipated his approaching death because he wrote his Last Will and Testament shown in Appendix IV on 7 January 1863, just twelve days before his death. If Benjamin had lived to see the end of the war, he surely would have remembered his welcome home as a hero in Wayne County, Kentucky during The Second War of America's Independence even though his militia company never fought the British and their Indian allies and he would have welcomed his two sons and his son-in-law home as heroes even though their country–his country–had lost the war for its independence.

"Though men deserve, they may not win, success:
The brave will honor the brave, vanquished none the less." [183]

BENJAMIN ELLIOTT JONES
6 March 1790–19 January 1863

AFTERWORD

The War of 1812 ended without a Winner, but there was a Loser. Although some in both the U.S. and Britain claimed that they won the war and some historians since have echoed their sentiments, neither side won the war. The Treaty of Ghent ending the war did not discuss any of the grievances causing the war. It simply restored relations between Britain and the U.S. and restored the borders of the two countries to the borders existing before the war. Both countries won notable victories in the war and both countries suffered notable defeats, but neither side won the war. The U.S. Navy proved that it could win one-on-one ship battles with the Royal Navy–the largest and most powerful navy in the world–but the British Navy maintained its supremacy during most of the war and shut down America's international trade by blockading America's ports, stopped privateering by American ships, and successfully attacked American towns and plantations along the Chesapeake Bay. The British successfully stopped repeated American efforts to invade Canada, but the British invasions of Louisiana, Maryland, and New York were defeated. Neither side won the war.

Although the British amassed a huge invasion force of veteran British troops in Canada, maintained naval supremacy throughout the war in the Atlantic, and there was an open American secessionist movement in New England, the British did not win the war. Although the Americans killed Tecumseh and broke his confederacy of Indian Tribes in the Northwest and Andrew Jackson defeated the Creeks in the Southeast and opened the way for American settlement on its frontiers, America did not win the war. Although Britain burned the Executive Mansion, the U.S. Capitol, the Treasury, and the U.S. War Office in Washington, it was defeated in the Battles of Baltimore, Fort McHenry, Plattsburg, and New Orleans and did not win the war.

Both sides suffered comparable casualties during the war, but neither side won the war. British losses, not including losses among its Canadian militia and Indian allies, included 1,160 killed in action, 3,679 wounded, 1,000 missing in action, and 3,321 dying from disease and accidents. American loses included 2,260 killed in action, 4,505 wounded, 695 missing in action, and an estimated 4,540 dying from disease and accidents.

American nationalism soared after its victory at New Orleans and Americans celebrated their assured independence from Britain in The Second War of America's Independence, but the Americans did not win the war. There was no Winner in the war, but there was a Loser.

The unquestioned Loser in the War of 1812 was the Native Americans who were abandoned by their British allies during the peace process. An Indian barrier State supported by the British was not created in the American Northwest Territory. The strength of the Indians was destroyed in both the Northwest and Southeast Territories; the Indians lost their fur-gathering and hunting territories; and the Indians suffered some 10,000 casualties in the war–the greatest number of casualties of any combatant in the war as a percentage of its population.

Although both Britain and the U.S. agreed in Article IX of the Treaty of Ghent to make peace with their indigenous foes and to restore Native peoples to "all possessions, rights, and privileges which they may have enjoyed, or been entitled to in 1811," the U. S. ignored this provision of the treaty and the British failed to require the Americans to honor it. The war left the Native Americans powerless and vulnerable. It hastened the loss of their traditional way of life and eventually resulted in the removal of most of the Indian tribes to the Indian Territory in the Southwest. There was no Winner in the War of 1812, but there was a Loser and the Loser was the Native Americans.

APPENDIX I

COMPANY CAPTAINS IN COLONEL JOSHUA BARBEE'S 7TH REGIMENT, KENTUCKY MILITIA[184]

James Barbee – Mercer County
William Cross – Cumberland County
Peter Jordan – Mercer County
David McNair – Cumberland County
Garret Peterson – Washington County
John Shelby – Adair County
Micah Taul – Wayne County

APPENDIX II

CAPTAIN MICHA TAUL'S COMPANY OF INFANTRY, SEVENTH REGIMENT, KENTUCKY MILITIA[185]

OFFICERS/STAFF:

Micah Taul, Captain
Joseph H. Woolfolk, Lieutenant
John Bartleson, Ensign
James Givens, First Sergeant
John Shannon, Fourth Sergent
John Dodson, First Corporal
Thomas C. Pemberton, Third Corporal
Noah Wilhite. Fourth Corporal
William Cowan, Drummer
Stephen Hines, Fifer

PRIVATES:

Esquire Baker	Samuel Ford	Daniel Peveyhouse	Valentine Worley
William Barnes	John Foster	John Ray	John Wright
Joshua Baxter	Anderson Garland	James Ridgeway	James Young
William Blair	John Garovir	John Roberts	
Welsher Buckhannon	Rodes Garth	Joab Rowe	
John Buster	Mordecai Gregory	George Rudd	
Lewis Coffey	William Hall	Richard Savage	
James Cotton	John Hicks	John Shrewsbury	
Edward N. Cullom	Parkman Howard	Jacob Souther	
Tillman Cullom	Samuel Ingraham	William Summers	
Alexander Davis	Augusta Johnson	Thomas Terrell	
Thomas Decker	**Benjamin Elliott Jones**	Moses Tucker	
John Dick	James Jones	John Tuller	
Soloman Dunagan	William Jones	Henry Tuttle	
Daniel East	James Langston	James Tuttle	
David East	James LeGrand	David Vestol	
North East	Cyrus Logan	Issac VanWinkle	
John Easter	William Miller	Micajah VanWinkle	
Walter Emerson	John Montgomery	Adam Vickery	
Samuel England	Jonathan Moore	Ballenger Wade	
Jesse Flinn	John M. Newell	Isaac West	

APPENDIX III

1860 U.S. FEDERAL CENSUS SLAVE SCHEDULES[186]

Name: **Benjamin Jones**

Residence: East Division, Fayette, Alabama, USA

Number of Enslaved People: 10

Gender	Age
Male	25
Female	24
Male	4
Male	2
Female	3/12
Female	3/12
Female	19
Female	4
Male	2
Male	10/12

APPENDIX IV

LAST WILL AND TESTAMENT BENJAMIN ELLIOTT JONES 7 JANUARY 1863[187]

THE STATE OF ALABAMA
FAYETTE COUNTY

I Benjamin Jones of said County being mindful of mortality do make & publish this my last will & testament. First, it is my will that I be decently & plainly buried without any pomp or show. Secondly, it is my will that my executor hereinafter appointed pay all my just debts & funeral expenses. Thirdly, it is my will that my negro woman Nina and her child I bequeath to my beloved son Elliott P Jones & that I bequeath to my daughter Frances Anne E Gaines wife of George S Gaines, Franklin & Becka & I bequeath to my son Robert G Jones my negro boy John and Jane to belong to my said children absolutely. It is my will that said negroes be valued by three disinterested men at a fair cash valuation & said children take them at the valuation. Fourthly, it is my will that my executor pay to my grand-daughter Sarah E. F. Jones, daughter of my deceased son Sylvester B Jones twenty-five dollars out of the monies arising from the sale of any property hereinafter mentioned, this amount to be her full share of my estate. Fifthly, it is my will that my said executor pay over to my daughter Eliza Jane Cole wife of Richard Cole the sum of three hundred dollars as her part of my estate. Sixthly, I further will and bequeath to my son Robert G. Jones all of my lands south of the creek to be his absolutely, he having settled & built & put up improvements on it. It is my will that my said executor hereafter appointed shall sell all of my personal property not otherwise disposed of every kind at public or private sale as he may think best, & on such time or for cash as he may think proper & the money arising from the sale of said property as well as the money on notes on hand after paying of the legacies heretofore mentioned to be applied as follows, First, in making up my dearly beloved wife Narcissa Jones & my son John W Jones equal with the valuation of the negroes aforesaid & after doing this to be divided between my wife aforesaid and my children John W., Robert G., Frances Anne E. Gaines, wife of George S. Gaines & Elliott P Jones intending to make these equal after giving Robert the lands mentioned aforesaid. Any of the property that my beloved wife may want she can keep at a fair price making her up equal with the children. Seventhly, it is my will further that the balance of my land remain for a home for my wife during her life if she desires to remain on it & at her death or whenever she wants to leave it I desire that my said executor sell the land as he may think best & the proceeds of said sale to be divided between my children John W., Elliott P., Robert G. & Frances Anne E. Gaines. Eighthly, it is my will that after this will is probated my executor be not required to give bond or make settlement with the court. That he proceed as soon as he can do so to pay off the legacies and take their receipts. I do this to save expenses. Ninthly, I hereby constitute and appoint my son Elliott P Jones my executor of this my last will. In testimony whereof I have hereunto set my hand, this the 7th day of January, 1863.

Benjamin Jones

Signed in each of our presence the same date.

John W. Whitson, Elvira M. Hill, Wm. H. (x) his mark Cornelius

Recorded: in Record 11, page 443

APPENDIX V

GENEALOGY OF
BENJAMIN ELLIOTT JONES[188]

EDWARD WADE, SR. married Jane Dorothy
Born 1611 in London, England
Migrated to the Virginia Colony in July 1635 aboard the ship "Paule"
Died December 1675 in the Virginia Colony

EDWARD WADE, JR married Mary Hampton
Born @ 1640 in the Virginia Colony Born @ 1652 in the Virginia Colony
Died before 1682 in the Virginia Colony Died 1700 in the Virginia Colony

JAMES WADE, SR. married Margaret Mosby
Born @ 1665 in the Virginia Colony
Died 1740 in the Virginia Colony

JOHN WADE married Elizabeth Dawson
Born @ 1704 in the Virginia Colony Born 1719 in the Virginia Colony
Died 2 July 1787 in Virginia

DAWSON WADE, SR. married Rachael Burnside
Born 1732 in the Virginia Colony Born 1735 in the Virginia Colony
Died 8 December 1819 in Montgomery Co., KY Died 1783 in Montgomery Co., KY

Rev. Elliott Jones married **ELIZABETH WADE**
Born 1764 in the Virginia Colony Born 1764 in the Virginia Colony
Died 16 December 1894 in Lawrence Co., AL Died 15 April 1856 in Lawrence Co. AL

BENJAMIN ELLIOTT JONES *married* Viney Wallace
Born 26 March 1790 in Kentucky Born 20 May 1792 in Kentucky
Died 19 January 1863 in Fayette Co., AL Died 19 August 1840 in Fayette Co., AL

About the Author

Gary C. Cole is an eleventh-generation American who is a lineal descendent of a representative of the Virginia General Assembly in 1629, a member of Virginia Governor Berkeley's Council in 1675-1692, Secretary of the Virginia Colony in 1689-1692, a Veteran of the French and Indian War of 1754-1763, four Veterans/Patriots of the Revolutionary War, a Veteran of the War of 1812, two citizens of the Republic of Texas, and three Confederate Veterans of the War for Southern Independence.

He was born in Dallas, Texas in 1943 and graduated Summa Cum Laude from Texas Christian University in 1965. He is a member of The Sons of the Republic of Texas and the Sons of Confederate Veterans. He has authored three books about the War for Southern Independence, this book about the War of 1812, and a book about the History of the Cole Family from the 13th Century.

He is a retired insurance company executive and served for seventeen years on the Board of Directors of the Texas Health Insurance Pool, including eleven years as its Chairman, Past Director of the Texas Legal Reserve Officials Association, Past President of the Texas Association of Life & Health Insurers, Past President of East Texas Association of Health Underwriters, a past member of the Board of Directors of Regions' Bank-Tyler, and a Past Director of the American Red Cross of Smith County. He is an ordained Baptist Deacon and lives in Tyler, Texas with his wife Jestine.

Illustration Credits

1812 U.S. Flag.
Melissa Strickland. Tyler, Texas 2022

Foreword
Jones Gravestone.
Deana Woolfolk Costner. Orlando, Florida 2014

Chapter 1
Upper & Lower Canada in 1791.
Gary C. Cole. Tyler, Texas 2022

Chapter 2
Detroit River.
Gary C. Cole. Tyler, Texas 2022

Chapter 4
Marriage Consent.
Kentucky County Marriage Records, 1783-1965.

Chapter 5
Wayne County, Kentucky.
Gary C. Cole. Tyler, Texas 2022

Chapter 6
Battle on Lake Erie.
Library of Congress. Reproduction Number LC-USZ62-27701

The Southern Frontier.
Gary C. Cole. Tyler, Texas 2022

Chapter 7
U.S. Capitol Burned By The British.
Library of Congress. Prints and Photographs Division
Washington, D.C. 20540 USA. Reproduction Number: LC-
DIG-ppmsca-23076

Chapter 8
Alabama.
Gary C. Cole. Tyler, Texas 2022

Back Cover
Author's Photograph.
Carrie R. Hall. Troup, Texas 2014

Endnotes

1 War of 1812. Wikipedia.https://en.wikipedia.org/w/index.php/
title=War_of_1812&oldid=948388203

2 Holmberg, Tom. *Great Britain: Orders in Council and Licenses
1800-1810.* www.napoleon-server.org/research/governmentbritish/c-
ordercouncil.html

3 *A Brief Overview of the War of 1812.* American Battlefield Trust.
www.battlefields.org.>learn/articles>brief-overview-war-1812

4 Holmberg, Tom. *Great Britain: Orders in Council and
Licenses1800-1810.* www.napoleon-server.org/research/government/
c-orderscouncil.html

5 *A Brief Overview of the War of 1812.* American Battlefield Trust.
www.battlefields.org>learn/articles>brief-overview-war-1812

6 *War of 1812.* Wikipedia. https://en.wikipedia.org/w/index.
php?title=War_of_1812&oldid=948388203

7 History.com Editors. *Treaty of Paris.* https://history.com/topics/
American-revolution/treaty-of-paris

8 *War of 1812.* Wikipedia. https://en.wikipedia.org/w/index.
php?title=War_of_1812&oldid=948388203

9 *War of 1812.* Wikipedia. https://en.wikipedia.org/w/index.
php?title=War_of_1812&oldid=948388203

10 *War of 1812.* Wikipedia. https://en.wikipedia.org/w/index.
php?title=War_of_1812&oldid=948388203

11 *USS Constitution vs HMS Guerriere.* Wikipedia. https://
en.wikipedia.org/index.php?title=USS_Constitution_vs_HMS_
Guerriere&oldid=950551833

12 Warshauer, Matthew. *The "Notorious" Hartford Convention.*
Connecticut Explored.Ctexplored.org/the-notorious-hartford-
convention

13 *William Hull.* Wikipedia. https://en.wikipedia.org/w/index.
php?title=William_Hull&oldid=942531566

14 *William Hull*. Wikipedia. https://en.wikipedia.org/w/index.php?title=William_Hull&oldid=942531566

15 *Fort Detroit*. https:en.wikipedia.org/w/index.php?title=Fort_Detroit&oldid=952668511

16 *William Hull*. Wikipedia. https://en.wikipedia.org/w/index.php?title=William_Hull&oldid=942531566

17 *William Hull*. Wikipedia. https://en.wikipedia.org/w/index.php?title=William_Hull&oldid+942531566

18 *Hull Attacks Canada*. History Central. centralhistory.com./1812/hull.html

19 *Fort Malden*. Wikipedia. https://en.wikipedia.org/w/index.php?title=Fort_Malden&oldid=946981167

20 Garcia, Bob. *Fort Amberstburg in the War of 1812*. Warof1812.ca/fortambg.htm

21 *Fort Malden*. Wikipedia. https://en.wikipedia.org/w/index.php?title=Fort_Malden&oldid=946981167

22 *Siege of Fort Mackinac*. Wikipedia. https://en.wikipedia.org/w/index.php?title=Siege_of_Fort_Mackinac&oldid=944633251

23 Coles, Harry L. *The War of 1812*. The University of Chicago Press. Chicago, Illinois 1965 p 58

24 *Siege of Fort Mackinac*. Wikipedia. https://en.wikipeda.org/w/indexphp?title=Siege_of_Fort_Mackinac&oldid=944633251

25 *Battle of Brownstown*. Wikipedia. https://en.wikipedia.org/w/index.php?title=Battle_of_Brownstown&oldid=928454009

26 Hickman, Kennedy. *War of 1812 Major General Sir Isaac Brook*. Thought Co. thought.com/major-general-sir-isaac-brock=2360138

27 *War of 1812*. Wikipedia. https://en.wikipedia.org/w/index/php?title=War_of_1812&oldid=948388203

28 Hickman,Kennedy. *War of 1812 Major General Sir Issac Brock*. Thought Co. thought.com/major-general-sir-issac-brock=2360138

29 Hickman, Kennedy. *War of 1812 Major General Sir Issac Brock*. Thought Co thought.com/major-general-sir-issac-brock=2360138

30 *William Hull*. Wikipedia. https://en.wikipedia.org/w/index.php?title=William_Hull&oldid=942531566

31 History.com Editors. *U.S. Surrenders Fort Detroit to the British*. https://www.history.com/this-day-in-history/detroit-surrenders-without-a-fight

32 *William Hull*. Wikipedia. https://en.wikipedia.org/w/index.php?title=William_Hull&oldid=943531566

33 *War of 1812*. Wikipedia. https://en.wikipedia.org/w/index.php?title=War_of_1812&oldid=948388203

34 William Hull. Wikipedia. https://en.wikipedia.org/w/index.php?title=William_Hull&oldid=942531566

35 History.com Editors. *U.S. Surrenders Fort Detroit to the British*. https://www.history.com/this-day-in-history/detroit-surrenders-without-a-fight

36 Everton, George B. *Handy Book for Genealogists*. The Everton Publishers, Inc. Logan, Utah 1969 p 86

37 *History of Kentucky*. Wikipedia. en.wikipedia.org>wiki>history>History_of_Kentucky

38 Everton, George B. *Handy Book for Genealogists*. The Everton Publishers, Inc. Logan, Utah 1969 p 87

39 *History of Kentucky*. Wikipedia. en.wikipedia.org>wiki>history>History_of_Kentucky

40 Costner, Deana Woolfolk. Orlando, Florida 20 July 2020

41 Everton, George B. *Handy Book for Genealogists*. The Everton Publishers, Inc. Logan, Utah 1967 p 86

42 Costner, Deana Woolfolk. Orlando, Florida 20 July 2020

43 Costner, Deana Woolfolk. Orlando, Florida 20 July 2020

44 Costner, Deana Woolfolk. Orlando, Florida 20 July 2020

45 Johnson, Augusta Phillips. *A Century of Wayne County Kentucky, 1800-1900*. Standard Printing Company, Incorporated. Louisville, Kentucky 1939

46 Costner, Deana Woolfolk. Orlando, Florida 20 July 2020

47 Johnson, Augusta Phillips. *A Century of Wayne County Kentucky, 1800-1900*. Standard Printing Company, Incorporated. Louisville, Kentucky 1939. Chapter III

48 *Narcissa Jones' War of 1812 Claim of Widow for Pension Application dated 2 August 1878*. Nancy Cole Douglas. Azle, Texas. October 2020

49 Johnson, Augusta Phillips. *A Century of Wayne County Kentucky, 1800-1900*. Standard Printing Company, Incorporated. Louisville, Kentucky 1939. Chapter III

50 Johnson, Augusta Phillips. *A Century of Wayne County Kentucky, 1800-1900*. Standard Printing Company, Incorporated. Louisville, Kentucky 1939

51 Coles, Harry L. *The War of 1812*. The University of Chicago Press. Chicago, Illinois 1965. p 112

52 Blum, Raymond K. *Battle of Tippecanoe*. www.britannica. com>event>Battle-of-Tippecanoe

53 Johnson, Augusta Phillips. *A Century of Wayne County Kentucky, 1800-1900*. Standard Printing Company, Incorporated. Louisville, Kentucky 1939. Chapter III

54 Johnson, Augusta Phillips. *A Century of Wayne County Kentucky, 1800-1900*. Standard Printing Company, Incorporated. Louisville, Kentucky 1939. Chapter III

55 Johnson, Augusta Phillips. *A Century of Wayne County Kentucky, 1800-1900*. Standard Printing Company, Incorporated. Louisville, Kentucky 1939. Chapter III

56 Johnson, Augusta Phillips. *A Century of Wayne County Kentucky, 1800-1900*. Standard Printing Company, Incorporated. Louisville, Kentucky 1939. Chapter III

57 *USS Constitution vs HMS Guerriere*. Wikipedia. https:// en.wikipedia.org/w/index/php?title=USS_Constitution_vs_HMS_ Guerriere&oldid=950551833

58 *USS Constitution vs HMS Guerriere*. Wikipedia. https:// en.wikipedia.org/w/index/php?title=USS_Constitution_vs_HMS_ Guerriere&oldid=950551833

59 *USS Constitution vs HMS Guerriere*. Wikipedia. https://
en.wikipedia.org/w/index/php?title=USS_Constitution_vs_HMS_
Guerriere&oldid=950551833

60 *USS Constitution vs HMS Guerriere*. Wikipedia. https://
en.wikipedia.org/w/index/php?title=USS_Constitution_vs_HMS_
Guerriere&oldid=950551833

61 Johnson, Augusta Phillips. *A Century of Wayne County Kentucky,
1800-1900*. Standard Printing Company, Incorporated. Louisville,
Kentucky 1939. Chapter III

62 *Memoirs of Micah Taul*. Kentucky Historical Society. Register of
Kentucky State Historical Society Vol. 27, No. 79 (January, 1929) p
372 https://www.jstor.org/stable/23370166

63 Greenspan, Jesse. *How U.S. Forces Failed to Conquer Canada 200
Years Ago*.

64 *Fort Piqua*. https://www.fortwiki.com/index.php?title=Fort_
Piqua&oldid=129739

65 Coles, Harry L. *The War of 1812*. The University of Chicago
Press. Chicago, Illinois 1965 p 113

66 Coles, Harry L. *The War of 1812*. The University of Chicago
Press. Chicago, Illinois 1965 p 113

67 Johnson, Augusta Phillips. *A Century of Wayne County Kentucky,
1800-1900*. Standard Printing Company, Incorporated. Louisville,
Kentucky 1939. Chapter III

68 *Siege of Fort Wayne*. Wikipedia. https:en.wikipedia.org/w/index.
php?title=Siege_of_Fort_Wayne&oldid=954513727

69 *Battle of Fallen Timbers*. https:en.wikipedia.org/w/index.
php?title=Battle_of_Fallen_Timbers&oldid=952621905

70 *Siege of Fort Wayne*. Wikipedia. https:en.wikipedia.org/w/index.
php?title=Siege_of_Fort_Wayne&oldid=954513727

71 Johnson, Augusta Phillips. *A Century of Wayne County Kentucky,
1800-1900*. Standard Printing Company, Incorporated. Louisville,
Kentucky 1939. Chapter III

72 *Fort Loramie*.fortwiki.com/Fort_Loramie

[73] Johnson, Augusta Phillips. *A Century of Wayne County Kentucky, 1800-1900*. Standard Printing Company, Incorporated. Louisville, Kentucky 1939. Chapter III

[74] *Fort St. Mary's Marker*. The Historical Database. hmdb.org/m.asp?m=19855

[75] Johnson, Augusta Phillips. *A Century of Wayne County Kentucky, 1800-1900*. Standard Printing Company, Incorporated. Louisville, Kentucky 1939. Chapter III

[76] Johnson, Augusta Phillips. *A Century of Wayne County Kentucky, 1800-1900*. Standard Printing Company, Incorporated. Louisville, Kentucky 1939. Chapter III

[77] *Fort Defiance (Ohio)*. https:en.wikipedia.org/w/index.php?title=Fort_Defiance(Ohio)&oldid=90718933

[78] Johnson, Augusta Phillips. *A Century of Wayne County Kentucky, 1800-1900*. Standard Printing Company, Incorporated. Louisville, Kentucky 1939. Chapter III

[79] Johnson, Augusta Phillips. *A Century of Wayne County Kentucky, 1800-1900*. Standard Printing Company, Incorporated. Louisville, Kentucky 1939. Chapter III

[80] Johnson, Augusta Phillips. *A Century of Wayne County Kentucky, 1800-1900*. Standard Printing Company, Incorporated. Louisville, Kentucky 1939. Chapter III

[81] *Fort Jennings Marker*. The Historical Marker Database. hmdb.org/m.asp?m=18782

[82] Martin, Evelyn. *This and That-The Fort of Fort Jennings*. August 14, 2016

[83] Johnson, Augusta Phillips. A Century of Wayne County Kentucky, 1800-1900. Standard Printing Company, Incorporated. Louisville, Kentucky 1939. Chapter III

[84] Johnson, Augusta Phillips. *A Century of Wayne County Kentucky 1800-1900*. Standard Printing Company, Incorporated. Lewisville, Kentucky 1939. Chapter III

[85] Johnson, Augusta Phillips. *A Century of Wayne County Kentucky, 1800-1900*. Standard Printing Company, Incorporated. Louisville, Kentucky 1939. Chapter III

[86] Johnson, Augusta Phillips. *A Century of Wayne County Kentucky 1800-1900*. Standard Printing Company, Incorporated. Lewisville, Kentucky 1939. Chapter III

[87] *Memoirs of Micah Taul*. Register of Kentucky State Historical Society Vol. 27, No. 79 (January, 1929) pp 372-374 https://www.jstor.org/stable/23370166

[88] *Battle of Queenston Heights*. Wikipedia. https://en.wikipedia.org/w/index.php?title=Battle_of_Queenston https:en.wikipedia.org/w/index.php?title=Battle_of_Queenston_Heights&oldid=950493624

[89] Richard, J. *United States vs Macedonian, 25 October 1812*. https://www.historyofwar/articles/battles_united_states_vs_macedonian.html

[90] *Memoirs of Micah Taul*. Register of Kentucky State Historical Society Vol. 27. No. 79 (January, 1939) p 375. https://www.jstor.org/stable/23370166

[91] *HMS Java (1811)*. Wikipedia. https://en.wikipedia.org/w/index.php?title=HMS_Java_(1811)&oldid=957982878

[92] *HMS Java (1811)*. Wikipedia. https://en.wikipedia.org/w/index.php?title=HMS_Java_(1811)&oldid=957982878

[93] *HMS Java Battle*. USS Constitution Museum. ussconstitutionmuseum.org>majorevents>the-hms-java

[94] Coles, Harry L. *The War of 1812*. The University of Chicago Press. Chicago, Illinois 1965 p 114

[95] Coles, Harry L. *The War of 1812*. The University of Chicago Press. Chicago, Illinois 1965 pp 114-115

[96] Coles, Harry L. *The War of 1812*. The University of Chicago Press. Chicago, Illinois 1965 p 115

[97] *Battle of Frenchtown*. Wikipedia. https://en.wikipedia.org/w/index.php?title=Battle_of_Frenchtown&oldid=955643541

98 *Battle of Frenchtown.* Wikipedia. https://en.wikipedia.org/w/
index.php?title=Battle_of_Frenchtown&oldid=955643541
99 *Battle of Frenchtown.* Wikipedia. https://en.wikipedia.org/w/
index.php?title=Battle_of_Frenchtown&oldid=955643541
100 *Battle of Ogdensburg.* Wikipedia. https://en.wikipedia.org/w/
index.php?title=Battle_of_Ogdensburg&oldid=948860271
101 *Memoirs of Micah Taul.* Register of Kentucky State Historical
Society Vol. 27 No. 79 (January, 1939) p 376. https://www.jstor.org/
stable/23370166
102 *Memoirs of Micah Taul.* Register of Kentucky State Historical
Society Vol. 27, No. 79 (January, 1939) pp 376-377. https://www.
jstor.org/stable/23370166
103 *War of 1812.* Wikipedia. https://en.wikipedia.org/w/index.
php?title=War_of_1812&oldid=948388203
104 *Second Battle of Sacket's Harbor.* Wikipedia. https://
en.wikipedia.org/w/index.php?title=Second_Battle_of_Sacket%27s_
Harbor&oldid=9485618751
105 *Battle of York.* Wikipedia. https://en.wikipedia.org/w/index.
php?title=Battle_of_York&oldid=959191776
106 *Battle of York.* Wikipedia. https://en.wikipedia.org/w/index.
php?title=Battle_of_York&oldid=959191776
107 *Siege of Fort Meigs.* Wikipedia. https://en.wikipedia.org/w/index.
php?title=Siege_of_Fort_Meigs&oldid=962286163
108 *Siege of Fort Meigs.* Wikipedia.
https://en.wikipedia.org.w/index,php?title=Siege_of_Fort_
Meigs&oldid=96228613
109 *Battle of York.* Wikipedia. https://en.wikipedia.org/w/index.
php?title=Battle_of_York&oldid=959191776
110 Neimeyer, Charles P. *The Chesapeake Campaign 1813-1814.*
Center of Military History United States Army. Washington, D.C.
2014
111 Neimeyer, Charles P. *The Chesapeake Campaign 1813-1814.* Center
of Military History United States Army. Washington, D.C. 2014

[112] Neimeyer, Charles P. *The Chesapeake Campaign 1813-1814*. Center of Military History United States Army. Washington, D.C. 2014

[113] *Battle of Fort George*. Wikipedia. https://en.wikipedia.org/w/index.php?title=Battle_of_Fort_George&oldid=951453238

[114] *Second Battle of Sacket's Harbor*. Wikipedia. https://en.wikipedia.org/w/index.php?title=Second_Battle_of_Sacket%27s_Harbor&oldid=948561875

[115] *Second Battle of Sacket's Harbor*. Wikipedia. https://en.wikipedia.org/w/index.php?title=Second_Battle_of_Sacket%27s_Harbor&oldid=948561875

[116] *Capture of USS Chesapeake*. Wikipedia. https://en.wikipedia.org/w/index.php?title=Capture_of_USS_Chesapeake&oldid=964464352

[117] Ridler, Jason. *Battle of Stoney Creek*. The Canadian Encyclopedia. www.thecanadianencyclopedia.ca>article>battle-of-stoney-creek

[118] *Battle of Craney Island*. Wikipedia. https://en.wikipedia.org/w/Index.php?title=Battle_of_Craney_Island&oldid=930801637

[119] *Battle of Beaver Dams*. Wikipedia. https://en.wikipedia.org/w/index.php?title=Battle_of_Beaver_Dams&oldid=965204961

[120] Flanders, Alan. *Craney Island Battle Led to Burning of Hampton*. The Virginia Pilot, 1991. Scholar.lib.vt.edu>Va-news>Va-Pilot>issues

[121] *Battle of St. Michael's*. Wikipedia. https://en.wikipedia.org/w/index.php?title=Battle_of_St._Michaels&oldid=956111840

[122] *Battle of Lake Erie*. Wikipedia. https://en.wikipedia.org/w/index.php?title=Battle_of_Lake_Erie&oldid=960225352

[123] *Battle of the Thames*. Wikipedia. https://en.wikipedia.org/w/index.php?title=Battle_of_the_Thames&oldid=958181879

[124] Lafferty, Renee. *Battle of Chateauguay*. The Canadian Encyclopedia. www.thecanadianencyclopedia.ca>battle-of-chateauguay

[125] Lafferty, Renee. *Battle of Chateauguay*. The Canadian Encyclopedia. www.thecanadianencyclopedia.ca>battle-of-chateauguay

126 Lafferty, Renee. *Battle of Chateauguay*. The Canadian Encyclopedia. www.thecanadianencyclopedia.ca>battle-of-chateauguay

127 Lafferty, Renee. *Battle of Chateauguay*. The Canadian Encyclopedia. www.thecanadianencyclopedia.ca>battle-of-chateauguay

128 *Capture of Fort Niagara*. Wikipedia. https://en.wikipedia.org/w/index.php?title=Capture_of_Fort_Niagara&oldid=953853425

129 *Battle of Buffalo*. Wikipedia. https://en.wikipedia.org/w/index.php?title=Battle_of_Buffalo&oldid=944915446

130 Coles, Harry L. *The War of 1812*. The University of Chicago Press. Chicago, Illinois 1965 pp 147-148

131 Coles, Harry L. *The War of 1812*. The University of Chicago Press. Chicago, Illinois 1965 p 193

132 Coles, Harry L. *The War of 1812*. The University of Chicago Press. Chicago, Illinois 1965 pp 193-194

133 Waselkov, Gregory A. *Fort Mims Battle and Massacre*. Encyclopedia of Alabama, 2017. encyclopediaof alabama.org>article

134 Coles, Harry L. *The War of 1812*. The University of Chicago Press. Chicago, Illinois 1965 pp 196-197

135 *Andrew Jackson*. Wikipedia. en.wikipedia.org>wiki>Andrew Jackson

136 *Davy Crockett*. Wikipedia. en.wikipedia.org/wiki/Davy_Crockett

137 *Sam Houston*. Wikipedia. en.wikipedia.org>Sam_Houston

138 *Fort Strother*. Wikipedia. https://en.wikipedia.org/w/index.php?title=Fort_Strother&oldid=977124991

139 *Battle of Talladega*. Wikipedia. https://en.wikipedia.org/w/index.php?title=Battle_of_Talladega&oldid=931196223

140 *Battle of Autosee*. Wikipedia. https://en.wikipedia.org/w/index.php?title=Battle_of_Autosee&oldid=936518221

141 *Chesapeake Campaign – April 23, 1813 to September 14, 1814*. American Battlefield Trust. battlefields.org/learn/chesapeake-campaign-april-23-1813-september-14-1814.

[142] *Battles of Emuckfaw and Enotachopo Creek.* Wikipedia. https://en.wikipedia.org/wiki/Andrew_Jackson

[143] *Battle of Horseshoe Bend (1814).* Wikipedia. https://en.wikipedia.org/w/index.php?title=Battle_of_Horseshoe_Bend(1814)&oldid=967247117

[144] *Treaty of Fontainebleau (1814).* Wikipedia. en.wikipedia.org/wiki/Treaty_of_Fontainebleau_(1814)

[145] *A Brief Overview of the War of 1812.* American Battlefield Trust. www.battlefields.org>learn>articles>brief-overview-war-1812

[146] *Battle of Chippawa.* Wikipedia. https://en.wikipedia.org/w/index.php?title=Battle_of_Chippawa&oldid=9657580

[147] *Capture of Fort Erie.* www.mywarof1812.com>bauls

[148] *Capture of Fort Erie.* Wikipedia. https://en.wikipedia.org/w/index.php?title=Capture_of_Fort_Erie&oldid=927529376

[149] *Battle of Chippawa.* Wikipedia. https://en.wikipedia.org/w/index.php?title=Battle_of_Chippawa&oldid=965758017

[150] *The Battle of Chippawa.* Niagarafallsinfo.com/niagara-falls-history/niagara-falls-municipal-history/the-war-of-1812/the-battle-of-chippawa

[151] *Battle of Lundy's Lane.* Wikipedia. https://en.wikipedia.org/w/index.php?title=Battle_of_Lundy's%27s_Lane&oldid=964147787

[152] *Battle of Lundy's Lane.* Wikipedia. https://en.wikipedia.org/w/index.php?title=Battle_of_Lundy's%27s_Lane&oldid=964147787

[153] *Treaty of Ghent.* Wikipedia. https://en.wikipedia.org/w/index.php?title=Treaty_of_Ghent&oldid=959511328

[154] *Treaty of Fort Jackson.* Wikipedia. https://en.wikipedia.org/w/index.php?title=Treaty_of_Fort_Jackson&oldid=960638260

[155] Devlin, Phillip R. *Stonington Came Under Attack Twice in August.* patch.com>connecticut>stonington-came-under-attack-twice-in-August

[156] Richard, J. *Battle of Bladensburg, 24 August 1814.* http://www.historyofwar.org/articles/battles_bladensburg.html

157 Glass, Andrew. *British troops land at Benedict, Maryland, Aug.19, 1814.*

158 *Battle of Bladensburg, 24 August 1814.* http://www.historyofwar. org/articles/battles_blandensburg.html

159 *Fort Washington Park Maryland.* nps.gov/fowa/learn/ historyculture/warburton.html

160 *Raid on Alexandria.* Wikipedia. https://en.wikipedia.org/w/index. php?title=Raid_on_Alexandria&oldid=931213266

161 History.com Editors. *Battle of Plattsburgh.* https://www.history. com/topics/war-of-1812/plattsburg-battle-of

162 *The Battle of Lake Champlain and the End of the War of 1812.* www.history.navy.mil>nhhc>brouse-by-topic>1812

163 Ridler, Jason. Battle of North Point. The Canadian Encyclopedia. www.thecanadianencyclopedia.ca>article>battle-of-north-point.

164 *Fort McHenry.* American Battlefield Trust. battlefields.org/learn/ war-1812/battles/fort-mchenry

165 Battle of Malcom's Mills. Wikipedia. https://en.wikipedia.org/w/ index.php?title=Battle_of_Malcom%27s_Mills&oldid=968653182

166 *Battle of Pensacola.* Wikipedia. https://en.wikipedia.org/w/index. php?title=Battle_of_Pensacola_(1814)&oldid=964884863

167 *Treaty of Ghent.* Wikipedia. https://en.wikipedia.org/w/index. php?title=Treaty_of_Ghent&oldid=959511328

168 *New Orleans Chalmette Plantation.* American Battlefield Trust. www.battlefields.org/learn/war-1812/battles/new-orleans

169 *New Orleans Chalmette Plantation.* American Battlefield Trust. www.battlefields.org/learn/war-1812/battles/new-orleans

170 *Treaty of Ghent.* Wikipedia. https://en.wikipedia.org/w/index. php?title=Treaty_of_Ghent&oldid=959511328

171 *Capture of HMS Cyane and HMS Levant.* Wikipedia. https:// en.wikipedia.org/w/index.php?title=Capture_of_HMS_Cyane_and_ HMS_Levant&oldid=954968548

172 *Capture of HMS Cyane and HMS Levant.* Wikipedia. https://

en.wikipedia.org/w/index.php?title=Capture_of_HMS_Cyane_and_HMS_Levant&oldid=954968548

[173] *Capture of HMS Cyane and HMS Levant.* Wikipedia. https://en.wikipedia.org/w/index.php?title=Capture_of_HMS_Cyane_and_HMS_Levant&oldid=954968548

[174] Costner, Deana Woolfolk. Orlando, Florida May 2020

[175] Everton, George B. Sr. *Handy Book for Genealogists.* The Everton Publishers, Inc. Logan, Utah 1967

[176] Costner, Deana Woolfolk. Orlando, Florida May 2020

[177] Costner, Deana Woolfolk. Orlando, Florida May 2020

[178] Costner, Deana Woolfolk. Orlando, Florida May 2020

[179] *1860 U.S. Federal Census.* Ancestry.com

[180] *1860 U.S. Federal Census-Slave Schedules.* Ancestry.com

[181] *1860 Agricultural Census Schedule.* Ancestry.com

[182] Costner, Deana Woolfolk. Orlando, Florida May 2020

[183] *Confederate Veteran.* Columbia, Tennessee. Volume 78, No. 5 September/October 2020

[184] Johnson, Augusta Phillips. A *Century of Wayne County Kentucky 1800-1900.* Standard Printing Company, Incorporated. Louisville, Kentucky 1939. Chapter III

[185] Johnson, Augusta Phillips. A *Century of Wayne County Kentucky, 1800-1900.* Standard Printing Company, Incorporated. Louisville, Kentucky 1939. Chapter III

[186] *1860 U.S. Federal Census-Slave Schedules.* Ancestry.com

[187] Costner, Deana Woolfolk. Orlando, Florida May 2020

[188] Costner, Deana Woolfolk. Orlando, Florida May 2020

Bibliography

BOOKS

A Century of Wayne County Kentucky, 1800-1900. Johnson, Augustus Phillips. Standard Printing Company, Incorporated. Louisville, Kentucky 1939.

Handy Book for Genealogists. Everton, George B. The Everton Publishers, Inc. Logan, Utah 1969

The Chesapeake Campaign 1813-1814. Center of Military History United States Army Washington, D.C. 2014.

The War of 1812. Coles, Harry L. The University of Chicago Press. Chicago, Illinois 1965

ONLINE SOURSES

A Brief Overview of the War of 1812. American Battlefield Trust. www.battlefields.org>learn/articles>brief-overview-war-1812

Andrew Jackson. Wikipedia. en.wikipedia.org>wiki>Andrew_Jackson

Battle of Autosee. Wikipedia. https://en.wikipedia.org/w/index.php?title=Battle_of_Autosee&oldid=936518221

Battle of Beaver Dams. Wikipedia. https://en.wikipedia.org/w/index.php?title=Battle_of_Beaver_Dams&oldid=965204961

Battle of Brownstown. Wikipedia. https://en.wikipedia.org/w/index.php?title=Battle_of_Brownstown&oldid=928454009

Battle of Buffalo. Wikipedia. https://en.wikipedia.org/w/index.php?=Battle_of_Buffalo&oldid=944915446

Battle of Chippawa. Wikipedia.
   https://en.wikipedia.org/w/index.php?title=Battle_of_
   Chippawa&oldid=9657580
Battle of Craney Island. Wikipedia.
   https://en.wikipedia.org/w/index.php?title=Battle_of_Craney_
   Island&oldid=930801637
Battle of Fallen Timbers.
   https://en.wikipedia.org/w/index.php?title=Battle_of_Fallen_
   Timbers&oldid=952621905
Battle of Fort George. Wikipedia.
   https://en.wikipedia.org/w/index.php?title=Battle_of_Fort_
   George&oldid=951453238
Battle of Frenchtown. Wikipedia.
   https://en.wikipedia.org/w/index.php?title=Battle_of_
   Frenchtown&oldid=955643541
Battle of Horseshoe Bend (1814). Wikipedia.
   https://en.wikipedia.org/w/index.php?title=Battle_of_Horseshoe_
   Bend(1814)&oldid=967247117
Battle of Lake Erie. Wikipedia.
   https://en.wikipedia.org/w/index.php?title=Battle_of_Lake_
   Erie&oldid=960225352
Battle of Lundy Lane. Wikipedia.
   https://en.wikipedia.org/w/index.php?title=Battle_of_
   Lundy's%27s_Lane&oldid=964147787
Battle of Malcom's Mills. Wikipedia.
   https://en.wikipedia.org/w/index.php?title=Battle_of_
   Malcom%27s_Mills&oldid=968653182
Battle of Ogdensburg. Wikipedia.
   https://en.wikipedia.org/w/index.php?title=Battle_of_
   Ogdensburg&oldid=948860271
Battle of Pensacola. Wikipedia.
   https://en.wikipedia.org/w/index.php?title=Battle_of_Pensacola_
   (1814)&oldid=964884863

Battle of Queenston Heights. Wikipedia.
   https://en.wikipedia.org/w/index.php?title=Battle_of_Queenston_
   Heights&oldid =950493624

Battle of St. Michael's. Wikipedia.
   https://en.wikipedia.org/w/index.php?title=Battle_of_St._
   Michaels&oldid=956111840

Battle of Talladega. Wikipedia.
   https://en.wikipedia.org/w/index.php?title=Battle_of_
   Talladega&oldid=931196223

Battle of the Thames. Wikipedia.
   https://en.wikipedia.org/w/index.php?title=Battle_of_the_
   Thames&oldid=95181879

Battle of York. Wikipedia.
   https://en.wikipedia.org/w/index.php?title=Battle_of_
   York&oldid=959191776

Battles of Emuckfaw and Enotacopo Creek. Wikipedia.
   https://en.wikipedia.org/wiki/Andrew_Jackson *Berlin Decree*.
   Wikipedia.
   https://en.wikipedia.org/w/index.php?title=Berlin_
   Decree&oldid=946985404

Capture of Fort Erie. Wikipedia.
   https://en.wikipedia.org/w/index.php?=Capture_of_Fort_
   Erie&oldid=927529376

Capture of HMS Cyane and HMS Levant. Wikipedia.
   https://en.wikipedia/org/w/index.php?title=Capture_of_HMS_
   Cyane_and_Levant&oldid=954968548

Capture of Fort Niagara. Wikipedia.
   https://en.wikipedia.org/w/index.php?title=Capture_of_Fort_
   Niagara&oldid=953853425

Capture of USS Chesapeake. Wikipedia.
   https://en.wikipedia.org/w/index.php?title=Capture_of_USS_
   Chesapeake&oldid=964464352

Davy Crockett. Wikipedia. en.wikipedia.org/wiki/Davy_Crockett

Fort Defiance (Ohio.)
    https://en.wikipedia.org/w/index.php?title=Fort_
    Defiance(Ohio)&oldid=90718933)
Fort Detroit. https://en.wikipedia.org/w/index.php?title=Fort_
Detroit&oldid=952668511
Fort Loramie. Fortwiki.com/Fort_Loramie
Fort Malden. Wikipedia.
    https://en.wikipedia.org/w/index.php?title=Fort_
    Malden&oldid=946981167
Fort Struther. Wikipedia.
    https://en.wikipedia.org/w/index.php?title=Fort_
    Struther&oldid=977124991
History of Kentucky. Wikipedia. en.wikipedia.org>wiki>history.
Fort Piqua. https://www.fortwiki.com/index.php?title=Fort_
Piqua&oldid=129739
Fort St. Mary's Marker. The Historical Database.hmdb/m.
asp?m=19855
HMS Java (1811). Wikipedia.
    https://en.wikipedia.org/w/index.php?title=HMS_Java_
    (1811)&oldid=957982878.
HMS Java Battle. USS Constitution Museum.
    ussconstitutionmuseum.org>major>events>the>hms>java
New Orleans Calmette Plantation. American Battlefield Trust.
    www.battlefields.org/learn/war-1812/battles/new-orleans
Raid on Alexandria. Wikipedia.
    https://en.wikipedia.org/w/index.php?title=Raid_on_
    Alexandria&oldid=931213266
Sam Houston. Wikipedia.en.wikipedia.org>Sam_Houston
Second Battle of Sacket's Harbor. Wikipedia.
    https://en.wikipedia.org/w/index.php?title=Second_Battle_of_
    Sacket%27s_Harbor&oldid=9485618751
Siege of Fort Wayne. Wikipedia.
    https://en.wikipedia.org/w/index.php?title=Siege_of_Fort_
    Wayne&oldid=954513727

Siege of Fort Mackinac. Wikipedia.
    https://en.wikipedia.org/w/index.php?title=Siege_of_Fort_
    Mackinac&oldid=944633251
Siege of Fort Meigs. Wikipedia.
    https://en.wikipedia.org/w/index.php?title=Siege_of_Fort_
    Meigs&oldid=962286163
Treaty of Fontainebleau (1814). Wikipedia.
    en.wikipedia.org/wiki/Treaty_of_Fontainebleau_(1814)
Treaty of Fort Jackson. Wikipedia.
    https://en.wikipedia.org/w/index.php?title=Treaty_of_Fort_
    Jackson&oldid=960638260
Treaty of Ghent. Wikipedia.
    https://en.wikipedia.org/w/index.php?title=Treaty_of_
    Ghent&oldid=959511328
Treaty of Paris. https://www.history.com/topics/American-
    revolution/treaty-of-paris
USS Constitution vs HMS Guerriere. Wikipedia.
    https://en.wikipedia.org/index.php?title=USS_Constitution_
    HMS_ Guerriere&oldid=950551833
War of 1812. Wikipedia.
    https://en.wikipedia.org/w/index.php?title=War_
    of_1812&oldid=948388203
William Hull. Wikipedia.
    https://en.wikipedia.org/index.php?title=William_
    Hull&oldid=942531566

ARTICLES and MANUSCRIPTS

Battle of Bladensburg, 24 August 1814. Richard, J.
    http://www.historyofwar.org/articles/battles_bladenburg.html
Battle of Chateauguay. Lafferty, Renee. The Canadian Encyclopedia.
Battle of North Point. Ridler, Jason. The Canadian Encyclopedia.
Battle of Plattsburg. History.com Editors.
    https://www.history.com/topics/war-of-1812/plattsburg-battle-of

Battle of Stoney Creek. Ridler, Jason. The Canadian Encyclopedia.

British Troops Land at Benedict, Maryland, Aug. 19, 1814. Glass, Andrew.

Chesapeake Campaign – April 23, 1813 to September 14, 1814. American Battlefield Trust.
   battlefields.org/learn/cheaspeake-campaign-april-23-1813-september-14-1814

Craney Island Battle Led to Burning of Hampton. Flanders, Alan. The Virginia Pilot, 1991.
   Scholar.libvt.edu>Va-news>Va-Pilot>issues

Daily Journal 24 August-16 October of Captain Micah Taul's Company of Infantry, Seventh Regiment, Kentucky Militia. Garth, Rodes. A Century of Wayne County Kentucky, 1800-1900. Standard Printing Company, Incorporated. Louisville, Kentucky 1939

Fort Amberstburg in the War of 1812. Garcia, Bob. Warof1812.ca/fortambg.htm

Fort McHenry. American Battlefield Trust. battlefields.org/learn/war-1812/battles/fortmchenry

Fort Mims Battle and Massacre. Waselkov, Gregory A. Encyclopedia of Alabama, 2017.
   encyclopediaofalabama.org>article

Great Britain: Orders in Council and Licenses 1800-1810. Holmberg, Tom. www.napololeon-server.org/research/government/british/c_council.html

Hull Attacks Canada. History Central. centralhistory/1812/hull.htmla

Memoirs Of Micah Taul. Kentucky Historical Society. Register of Kentucky Historical Society Vol. 27, No.79 (January 1929)
   https://www.jstor.org/stable/23370166

Stonington Came Under Attack Twice in August. Devlin, Phillip R.
   patch.com>connenticut>stonington-came-under-attack-twice-in-August

This and That-The Fort of Fort Jennings, August 14, 2016. Martin, Evelyn.

United States vs Macedonian, 25 October 1812. Richard, J.
    https://www.historyofwar/articles/battles_united_states_vs_
    macedonian.html
U.S. Surrenders Fort Detroit to the British. History.com Editors.
    https://www.history.com/this-day-in history/detroit-surrenders-
    without-a-fight
War of 1812 Major General Sir Isaac Brook. Hickman, Kennedy.
Thought Co.
    thought.com/major-general-sir-isaac-brock=2360138

GOVERNMENT DOCUMENTS

1860 Agricultural Census Schedule
1860 U.S. Federal Census
1860 U.S. Federal Census Slave Schedules

OTHER RECORDS

Confederate Veteran. Columbia, Tennessee. Vol. 78, No. 5
September/October 2020
Costner, Deana Woolfolk. Orlando, Florida May 2020
Kentucky County Marriage Records, 1783-1965.
*Narcissa Jones' War of 1812 Claim of Widow for Pension
Application dated 2 August 1878.*
    Nancy Cole Douglas. Azle, Texas. October 2020